# ROLEMAPS

**The Instructional Design Library**

*Volume 33*

# ROLEMAPS

**Diane Dormant**
*Training and Instructional Systems Consultant*
*Bloomington, Indiana*

Danny G. Langdon
*Series Editor*

**Educational Technology Publications**
**Englewood Cliffs, New Jersey 07632**

✓

**Library of Congress Cataloging in Publication Data**

Dormant, Diane.
    Rolemaps.

    (The Instructional design library; v. 33)
    Bibliography: p.
    1. Role playing. 2. Education—Simulation methods.
I. Title. II. Series: Instructional design library;
v. 33.
LB1069.D64    371.3    79-23398
ISBN 0-87778-153-2

Printed in the United States of America.

Library of Congress Catalog Card Number:
79-23398.

International Standard Book Number:
0-87778-153-2.

First Printing: March, 1980.

# FOREWORD

One of the first things you will come to appreciate about Rolemaps is that it takes much of the mystery out of role playing. The reader will particularly appreciate the guidelines given in the Developmental Guide chapter for producing a Rolemap.

One of the most interesting design components of Rolemaps is the use of an audiotape for program control and presentation. Audio serves as an excellent time control means, thus bringing about efficient use of time by participants in the role play. Combined with role descriptions in booklets, the audio also assures uniform implementation—a useful feature for initial developmental tryout, continuous use, and validation. This allows the facilitator (instructor, workshop leader, etc.) to carefully observe group interaction dynamics.

For those of us who have tried role plays and felt an uncertainty in what we were doing and what resulted, Rolemaps are a welcome addition to making role plays easier on ourselves and our students.

Danny G. Langdon
Series Editor

# PREFACE

My thanks to Danny G. Langdon for inviting me to contribute to The Instructional Design Library. My thanks to Sivasailam (Thiagi) Thiagarajan for introducing me to so many professional opportunities and for saying, "Write, Diane, write." My thanks to Kathy Byers for reading an early version. And, my thanks most of all to Howard Levie for his conceptual and editorial assistance and for his patience and consistent encouragement.

D.D.

# CONTENTS

# ABSTRACT

## ROLEMAPS

A Rolemap is a systematically developed instructional activity involving structured role plays in a series of simulated situations. The role plays and the simulated situations are designed to reflect critical aspects of a central, controversial issue. Rolemaps are designed for small-group use, although several groups can work simultaneously. Rolemaps are usually presented by a workshop leader through a combination of printed booklets and audiotape. The Rolemap activity is followed by a carefully designed debriefing session. Rolemaps can be used with almost any central issue and virtually any age group. The specific instructional uses of Rolemaps include the following: to facilitate positive, active involvement in the learning process itself, to reveal different opinions and attitudes toward an issue, and to increase understanding and acceptance of divergent views toward an issue. The development of a Rolemap includes pre-design activities (e.g., analysis of the issue, statement of objectives), design activities (e.g., specification of sessions and roles, writing the script), and production activities (e.g., preparing the final audiotape and booklets, preparing the leader's guide).

# ROLEMAPS

# I.

# USE

**An Example**

If you were to observe a Rolemap in actual use, you might see something like this:

*Twenty-five workshop participants are seated around tables in groups of five or six. People seem to be doing the same thing at every table. For example, all participants are holding booklets and wearing name tags which prominently indicate role names and associated job titles (e.g., J. Marshall, Head of Marketing). From time to time, players refer to their individual booklets to get more information about their roles. However, most of the time, they are enthusiastically involved in discussion.*

*And, at each table, one person behaves a bit differently from the others. Although generally quiet, this person seems to be in charge. Also, occasionally, an audiotape recording comes on and gives information about various events associated with the topic under discussion, sometimes instructing players to change roles as they "go to" a new meeting.*

*After several discussion sessions, the audiotape announces that the Rolemap is at an end, and the time has come to return to the "real world" for a period of debriefing. With this, the workshop leader takes over and leads the participants through a series of questions.*

### Definition

A Rolemap is a systematically developed instructional activity involving structured role plays in a series of simulated situations. The role plays and the simulated situations are designed to reflect critical aspects of a central, controversial issue.

Rolemaps are designed for small-group use and are usually presented by a workshop leader* through a combination of printed booklets and audiotape. The audiotape sets up the scenario for sessions, gives instructions to the players, and acts as a timekeeper through the series of simulated situations or sessions. Participants learn about their individual roles through role descriptions which are given in individual booklets. Each role-play session is designed to reveal different perspectives on the central issue and is balanced across perspectives to stimulate debate. Upon completion of all sessions, the leader facilitates debriefing, which consists first of a spontaneous sharing of feelings and, then, of the systematic elicitation and clarification of the major points and relationships identified as important during the content analysis.

### Instructional Uses of Rolemaps

A Rolemap can be used with any subject matter or central issue, provided it is relevant to the participants, it involves a variety of viewpoints, and it lends itself to discussion. A Rolemap can be used with any age group which is capable of understanding written instructions and playing roles. While Rolemaps are designed for use by small groups (usually five or six persons), several such groups can simultaneously use a

---

*Rolemaps may be useful in a variety of instructional situations, e.g., as the major activity for one class meeting in a semester-long class or for a mutually-chosen activity in a voluntary study group. However, in this book, for simplicity's sake, the workshop and the workshop leader will be used as representative of the range of applications.

single Rolemap provided that multiple sets of materials are available. Although well-designed Rolemaps supported by effective debriefing sessions can stand alone, they are most frequently used as a part of some larger instructional program, such as a comprehensive workshop or a series of training sessions.

The specific instructional uses of Rolemaps are at least three: (1) to facilitate positive, active involvement in the learning process itself, (2) to reveal different opinions and attitudes toward an issue and its sub-issues, and (3) to increase understanding and acceptance of divergent views toward an issue.

*Facilitating positive, active involvement of participants.* Rolemaps, like role playing, tend to encourage participants to become active—toward the topic, toward each other, and toward the workshop leader. Instructional designers caution that "Role playing should not be attempted until the members of the group are familiar and friendly with each other" (Kozma, Belle, and Williams, 1978, p. 252). However, because of their controlled structure, this appears *not* to be a limitation of Rolemaps. In fact, in actual practice, it has been observed that—through participation in a Rolemap—people who do not know each other can rapidly develop interactive relationships. Moreover, the Rolemap may set the instructional tone for what is to follow. The communication patterns among group members and between them and the leader tend to be changed—opened up—as a result of a Rolemap activity. Also, the active character of the Rolemap involves participants in the learning situation, which facilitates positive attitudes and a willingness to share the responsibility for their own learning.

*Revealing different opinions and attitudes toward an issue.* A Rolemap is built around a controversial and complex issue. Prior to actual Rolemap design, this issue is analyzed for the purpose of identifying critical viewpoints, that is, sub-issues and related opinions and attitudes. When compared to trainee characteristics, these form the basis for the Rolemap's specific instructional objectives. And, since the Rolemap structure is specifically designed to reflect the various viewpoints on an issue, the results of the analysis also determine the roles and the role-play sessions of the Rolemap itself.

*Increasing understanding and acceptance of divergent views toward an issue.* In a typical Rolemap, a participant plays different types of roles during the sessions. These roles are based on real-world models who hold significant opinions and attitudes toward the issue being studied. In order to simulate real-world differences and to stimulate useful discussion, roles are assigned deliberately so that participants can explore and compare the feelings and views of various significant people. As they try to justify their role position to others, they tend to gain in understanding and empathy. Debriefing provides further clarification and an opportunity to plan for relevant real-world action.

**Caveats**

*Positive feedback can be misleading.* Most participants enjoy Rolemaps and, through their behavior during the activity as well as their comments afterward, provide the workshop leader with considerable positive feedback. While this is pleasant, the leader and the designer need to be aware that such "good feelings" may or may not accompany the achievement of the desired instructional objectives.

*Participants must "bring" something to the activity.* Any Rolemap which is appropriate to a given target population is necessarily concerned with an issue of importance to that population. Hence, in general, all participants can be expected to have some information on the issue under study. However, the more extensive the information and experience which the participants as a group have on the issues, opinions, attitudes, situations, and significant people, the more likely that the role-play discussions will be rich in relevant detail and useful in achieving instructional objectives.

## References

Janis, I.L., and Mann, L. Effectiveness of Emotional Role Playing in Modifying Smoking Habits and Attitudes. *Journal of Experimental Research in Personality,* 1965, 84-90.

Kozma, R.B., Belle, L.W., and Williams, G.W. *Instructional Techniques in Higher Education.* Englewood Cliffs, N.J.: Educational Technology Publications, 1978.

# II.

# OPERATIONAL DESCRIPTION

**Why a "Rolemap"?**

Rolemap is the name given to this instructional design because it relies heavily on *role playing* and because its structure reflects an analytical *mapping* of the content domain. This combination gives the Rolemap capabilities for implementing both affective and cognitive instructional objectives.

*Affective objectives.* Role plays are well-known for their strengths in affective areas, e.g., in eliciting empathetic responses, in influencing attitudes and associated behavior, and in encouraging active participation in learning. For example, while smoking is known to be an almost intractable behavior, one role play—during which participants play the roles of people who are shown X-rays, informed that they have lung cancer, and instructed in appropriate preparations for surgery—has resulted in the participants significantly reducing their smoking behavior (Janis, 1965). However, while such dramatic and desirable results are possible, role plays sometimes have equally dramatic but undesirable results. For example, one role play which involves an end-of-the-world simulation left some players hysterical. Because of such outcomes, teachers and trainers sometimes avoid role plays altogether. Rolemaps, however—with their carefully designed structure—preserve the utility and impact of role plays while reducing unpredictability.

*Cognitive objectives.* During the pre-design or analytical phase of development, the content domain or issue is analyzed to identify various critical sub-issues, opinions and attitudes, relevant situations, and significant people. The structure and content of the Rolemap's sessions and roles are correlated with the results of the content or issue analysis. For example, a Rolemap was developed for a teacher training workshop on the central issue of the integration of handicapped children into regular classrooms (mainstreaming). During the analysis phase of the development, several sub-issues were identified as being particularly important to the participants: a set of moralistic-humanistic issues; questions about budgeting and financial responsibility; and problems related to a regular classroom teacher's ability to provide handicapped children with effective instruction. Each of these sub-issues became the focus for one session of the Rolemap, and people who could logically present various perspectives of each sub-issue were identified and written into the roles. Hence, cognitive objectives related to the central issue are directly implemented in the design of a Rolemap.

### What Is a Rolemap?

As indicated in Chapter I, a Rolemap is a systematically developed instructional activity involving structured role plays in a series of simulated situations. It is designed for small-group use and is usually presented by a *workshop leader* through a combination of printed booklets and audiotape. The leader's role is two-fold: materials manager and debriefing facilitator. (And, also, if the audiotape equipment fails, the leader can take over and read from a script.)

The *audiotape* provides the scenario for each session, gives general instructions to players, and acts as a timekeeper through the series of Rolemap sessions. An audiotape control is recommended for a number of reasons: (1) it frees the leader to do other things, e.g., to clarify instructions, to make unobtrusive observations for subsequent use in debriefing or other follow-up activities, and to note revisions to be made in the Rolemap materials; (2) it provides a completely replicable activity, except for the debriefing period; (3) it is viewed by some participants as less disruptive and punitive than a human "timer"; and (4) it adds mediated interest to the activity (and can, in fact, be combined with pictures* for additional impact).

Participants learn about their individual roles through role descriptions which are given in *individual booklets.* Each participant has a different booklet, which only he or she sees and which provides information about the *role,* e.g., name, job title, general attitude toward issue, position on relevant sub-issues, relevant interests, reason for being at meeting, etc.

Each *session* is designed to reveal different opinions and attitudes toward various aspects of the issue and is balanced across these to stimulate debate. In order to keep the discussion moving, one participant (a different one for each session) is assigned the role of *neutral facilitator* and told to encourage others to express themselves.

Upon completion of all sessions, the workshop leader conducts a *debriefing period.* First, there is a cathartic phase in which people are invited, though not pressured, to respond to such a simple question as, "Would anyone like to share any feelings you had during the role plays?" This may result in nothing or something, e.g., "I didn't agree with the person I was playing, but I really got into it"; "I feel very discouraged since I really don't see any way to overcome feelings like those of the person I was playing"; "I've always been a little afraid to do things like this, but it was kind of fun." This spontaneous, sharing phase of debriefing is

*See *Kenny* in Appendix A.

followed by a carefully designed series of questions intended to elicit important comparisons—of the various sub-issues, of opinions and attitudes of significant people, of situational variables—and to lead to suggestions for real-world actions. Should the elicited responses not cover the pre-determined, salient points (instructional objectives), the leader may need to use leading questions or even make the points didactically.

**An Example**

A Rolemap is appropriate for a group of people who have a common concern about a central issue. They don't need to have identical backgrounds, but each should have experience and information which are relevant. For example, such a group was brought together in a two-day workshop for the training department of a hospital management corporation.

The corporation was in the process of introducing new management systems (e.g., data processing, business office procedures, inventory control) into its hospitals, and the training department had the task of training hospital personnel in the use of the new systems. The outside consultants (who designed the workshop) had determined that there was a variety of problems associated with such training and systems implementation. For example, the perspectives of the systems designers in corporate headquarters and those of the field personnel in the hospitals were quite divergent. Also, even with the field personnel, there were differences dependent upon the size of the hospital, the sophistication of personnel, and so forth. All members of the training department had past experience with hospital personnel, although some trainers had been assigned only to large, urban hospitals, while others had served smaller hospitals in low-population areas. Recently, several trainers had spent considerable time with various systems designers in an effort to assess the situation from the viewpoint of the systems designers or "content experts." In short, the members of the training department were—as a group—well qualified to engage in meaningful role playing and debriefing discussion— in a Rolemap called *The Caduceus\* Crisis.*

### How a Rolemap Begins

The workshop participants were arranged in groups of five and told that their next activity would be directed by an audiotape. The audiotape was then turned on and the narrator began, *Hello. Welcome to this workshop event,* and went on to set up the role-play activity:

*As the story opens, we are in the corporate headquarters of the Caduceus Corporation, a nationwide hospital management corporation. J. Peters, Executive Vice President, is presiding over a meeting. Four others are also in attendance.*

The narrator then introduced two "systems designers from corporate headquarters" and two "administrators from member hospitals," and went on:

*Recently the President of Caduceus sent a memo to the chief administrators of all member hospitals saying that they must adopt a new data processing system developed by Caduceus. Since the time his memo went out, he's received numerous complaints from hospital personnel across the nation. At the last Board meeting, it was decided that this whole issue of implementing management systems needed looking into. J. Peters, the Executive Vice President of Caduceus, was given the job and has called the meeting today just to gather information about this problem. Each of you was invited because Peters felt you might offer relevant information and opinions.*

### How the Action Proceeds

After the booklets were passed out to the participants, the audiotape continued:

---

*The "caduceus" is the insignia often used to symbolize the medical profession: it is a shaft with two entwined serpents and wings at the top.

*Open your booklets to Session I so you can see who you are and what you are like. One of you is J. Peters. When ready, Peters will call the meeting to order.*

And so it went through four sessions. These sessions—introduced and timed by the audiotape—directed each workshop participant to assume various corporate and hospital personnel roles. For example, in Session III, one participant played the role of J. Dionne, the Controller of a small, rural hospital which was sold to Caduceus after the death of its local doctor owner. Dionne hates the intrusion of "the big city boys who can't seem to understand the problems of a small hospital." In the same session, another participant plays the role of V. Artale, the newly appointed controller of a large city hospital which has suffered from poor management. Artale has worked in other large corporations and knows that a well-designed system can do a lot for an organization. Artale welcomes help from headquarters. Throughout the Rolemap, such realistic but contrasting points of view are revealed through the roles.

### What Happens After a Rolemap?

During the Rolemap, the participants—drawing upon their real-world experience in the corporate system—became more and more enthusiastically involved in playing their roles. By the time the audiotape narrator turned control over to the workshop leader for debriefing, they were eager to share their feelings and thoughts. "You know," one sophisticated trainer said chuckling, "I'm surprised at how much I enjoyed playing the role of Higgens—that stubborn, opinionated bumpkin. I'm not like that at all, but it sure was fun." Another said, "I have the corporate perspective and I know it, and when I'm out in the field I sometimes lose patience with the narrowness of the viewpoints of some of the hospital personnel. Still, when I was playing the role of that fellow Dionne, I really felt sympathy for his position. I mean, most of his life he's gone along doing just fine in that small community where everybody knows everybody else—and is probably related to them—and suddenly, the rug is pulled out from under him. His hospital is sold to some inanimate big business in Chicago. Why wouldn't the man be unhappy? And scared too!"

Initial questions on the part of the workshop leader which are intended to elicit such free, cathartic responses are usually advisable in the first phase of debriefing. The leader must be prepared, of course, for the possibility that no one has any "pent-up" feelings. But, if they do, and the leader presses on too soon to the content-oriented instructional questions, such feelings may surface and distract from subsequent content discussions.

However, once participants have had a chance to "get it out of their systems" (note that "it" may be positive as well as negative), the leader's questions will reflect the significant content analysis and the related instructional objectives. For example, some of the debriefing questions used in this workshop were:

- *Players A and E played roles of both small and large hospital personnel. Would those of you who were Players A or E respond to this question: What were the critical differences in perspective between small and large hospital personnel?*
- *Player B played only small hospital personnel; yet the two roles differed in opinion as to the "goodness" of management systems. What factors seem to make for this difference?*
- *Everyone played the role of a systems designer. What factors seem correlated with a positive attitude toward implementing management systems in the hospitals? With a negative attitude?*
- *If you were asked to write a set of guidelines for implementing management systems in the member*

*hospitals, what would be your DO's and DON'T's?
Let's list them on the chalkboard.*

The above questions represent only a sample of those used to guide the debriefing discussion. The entire list of questions reflects the stated instructional objectives and was first prepared—in rough draft—prior to the design and development of the Rolemap itself.

### The Designer's Matrix of a Rolemap

Figure 1 displays the role-session structure of this Rolemap. This matrix was used in the development of *The Caduceus Crisis*. The players or workshop participants are listed down the left side (A through F). The sessions are listed across the top (I through IV), along with a short statement of the major issue and meeting locale.

Each player's general attitude toward the issue (plus, minus, or zero for the neutral facilitator) is indicated for each session. This is a mechanical, but important, step in designing a functional Rolemap. If all players hold the same opinion, little conflict or useful discussion will occur. Usually, the best discussion results from having a balance of contrasting perspectives. Each session also needs someone (such as J. Peters in Session I) to play a neutral, facilitative role. And—although there are exceptions to this—Rolemaps tend to be more interesting if the participants get to play different kinds of roles. For example, looking across Player B's row, we see that in Session I he or she plays J. Rodriguez, Head of Systems Division, who is positive (plus). However, in Session II, Player B plays V. Greco, who as Chief Corporate Trainer is the neutral facilitator (zero). And, in Session III, Player B plays W. Higgens, Inventory Manager of the small Mt. Sinus Hospital, who is negative (minus). Last, in Session IV, Player B plays M. Brown, the Administrator of the small, N. Central Hospital, who is positive (plus). In addition to such a simple balance of attitudes, roles can be balanced in each session

## Figure 1

## THE CADUCEUS CRISIS: Design Matrix

| | SESSION I — Chicago Corp. Hdqrts. Role of "gatekeepers" in implementation | SESSION II — Chicago Corp. Hdqrts. Implementation probs. from various systems designers' viewpoints | SESSION III — Houston Regional Off. Implementation probs. from various hospital users' viewpoints | SESSION IV — Chicago Corp. Hdqrts. Multiple concerns which training must take into consideration |
|---|---|---|---|---|
| **A** | O — J. Peters, Exec. Vice Pres. | │ — S. Greenburg, Systems Designer | + — J. Dionne, Controller Mt. Sinus Hosp. (small) | │ — H. King, Administrator County Hosp. (large) |
| **B** | + — J. Rodriguez, Head of Systems Div. | O — V. Greco, Chief Corp. Trainer | │ — W. Higgens, Inventory Mgr. Mt. Sinus Hosp. (small) | + — M. Brown, Administrator N. Central Hosp. (small) |
| **C** | │ — G. Spock, Systems Designer | + — C. Mason, Systems Designer | O — V. Greco, Chief Corp. Trainer | │ — J. Rodriguez, Head of Systems Div. |
| **D** | + — H. King, Administrator County Hosp. (large) | │ — D. Jacobs, Systems Designer | + — E. Lee, Head Accountant Pacemaker Hosp. (large) | O — J. Peters, Exec. Vice Pres. |
| **E** | │ — M. Brown, Administrator N. Central Hosp. (small) | + — F. Chase, Systems Designer | │ — V. Artale, Controller Pacemaker Hosp. (large) | + — V. Greco, Chief Corp. Trainer |
| **F*** | + — B. Thompson, Administrator Interfaith Hosp. (medium) | │ — A. Smith, Systems Designer | + — P. O'Neal, Nurse Pacemaker Hosp. (large) | │ — B. Reston, Administrator Stony Road Hosp. (small) |

*Player F, a sixth player, is included to provide flexibility in actual use. This optional player should not be necessary to or distract from the action of the Rolemap.

across a number of different sub-issues. The more complex (and similar to the real world) the balancing of multiple issues becomes, the more necessary it is to have a systematic way to keep track.

# III.

# DESIGN FORMAT

The preceding chapters presented Rolemaps in a chrono-logical order, i.e., the beginning, the role-play sessions, and the conclusion of a typical Rolemap. This chapter—while still consistent with chronology—emphasizes (1) the various elements of a Rolemap and (2) their relationship to the central issue.

## The Elements of a Rolemap

The elements of a Rolemap include the following:
- an introduction;
- set-ups for each session;
- role descriptions for each session;
- role-playing sessions;
- closing comments; and
- debriefing.

These elements are described and illustrated below through examples from another Rolemap—*Screaming Committees.* This is a two-session Rolemap dealing with the topic of the selection of instructional materials in the public schools.*

*Screaming Committees* was developed as one module in the Educational Products Information Exchange Institute's Selection Training Package, 1978. *Screaming Committees,* Copyright © 1978 by EPIE Institute, is used here with the permission of EPIE Institute, 475 Riverside Drive, New York, New York 10027.

*Introduction*

Before a participant can be expected to participate in a Rolemap, some introduction is necessary. The participant needs to be oriented to (1) the Rolemap activity itself and (2) the central issue under consideration in the Rolemap. This is done through an audiotaped narration, as illustrated in this excerpt from *Screaming Committees*:

*Welcome to this workshop event. I'm going to be your narrator through a simulation. This simulation concerns the selection of textbooks in the Lincoln County School District. As we proceed, you'll be playing the roles of different people in the community. Some of you will be school administrators or teachers. Others will be parents or community leaders. This audiotape will give you specific instructions on what to do and when to do it. You will need to listen carefully.*

This brief introduction includes information on what kind of activity the participants are going to be engaged in, what sort of behavior is expected of them, and what they can expect from the audiotape component. In addition to such methodological information, the introduction includes information on the topic to be considered, i.e., the selection of textbooks in a given school district. An introduction can be as brief as this one, or it can be more elaborate—depending upon the learners, the situation, and the instructional objectives. For example, one Rolemap, *Kenny,* is introduced by a short audio-filmstrip (see Appendix A).

*Set-ups for Each Session*

Sessions are, in fact, simulated meetings where discussions can occur. For such meetings to have meaning to the participants, they must be adequately introduced or set up. Participants must be oriented to the situation represented in each session. For example, a session set-up would probably include all of the following information: what the occasion for the meeting is, who called it, where it is being held, what the discussion will focus on, and who the leader of the meeting will be. Each session needs such an orientation, and it is handled by the audiotape. The set-up for Session I is usually just a continuation of the general introduction. For example, in *Screaming Committees,* the narration continues on from that quoted above:

*First, let's find out with what kind of situation we're dealing. As the story opens, we are in the Administration Building of the Lincoln County School District. A committee is meeting for the first time this school year. It's a textbook selection committee with the task of selecting a science textbook series for grades one through eight. In Lincoln County, textbooks are adopted for five-year periods, and different subject areas are selected each year. For example, last year it was language arts.*

*The chairperson of this committee is Dr. Sanford. As the Director of Curriculum, Sanford has for many years coordinated textbook selection for elementary and middle schools. However, since last year, Sanford has had some new thoughts on selection. At a professional convention a few months ago, several presentations dealt with textbook selection and raised some questions about the usual information base for selection. Recalling that last year's committee was often frustrated by gaps in information, as well as by inconsistent information, Sanford is handling things a bit differently this year. Before the committee develops any specific criteria, or discusses any specific textbook series, Sanford wants them to spend some time discussing what kind of information they want and need.*

*Including Sanford, this year's committee consists of five people. One of them, McCullough, is the principal of a suburban middle school. Navarro and Kent are teachers—one from elementary and one from high school. And, in keeping with the current effort to involve parents, one member, Boyd, is a parent who has agreed to serve on the committee.*

*None of the committee members has ever met one another before.*

*As the committee meets this first time, each of you will take on one of the committee member roles. One of you will be Sanford, who will facilitate this first meeting. One of you will be McCullough, the middle school principal. Two will be the teachers, Navarro and Kent. And one will be Boyd, the parent.*

*In a few minutes, the workshop leader will give you a rolecard. You'll find out who you are and what kind of attitude you have toward textbook selection in general—and science textbooks in particular. Then, based on your role and your attitude, you'll be making a case for the kind of information you think is important in the selection of a science textbook series. Remember, you are not setting up criteria for selecting textbooks but merely listing the different types of information you need.*

*When you get your rolecard, fold the card and set it up in front of you so that the others can see your name and job title in large print and so you can see your role and instructions in smaller print. After your card is set up, read your role carefully and think about yourself. What kind of a person are you? When Sanford begins the meeting, be prepared to introduce yourself to the group.*

*Workshop Leader—Please distribute the cards and demonstrate how to set them up.*

This set-up to Session I ended as they usually do, that is, with instructions to the participants to turn to their individual sources (booklets or rolecards) for information on their individual roles in Session I.

Set-ups, like other audiotaped information, should be in easily understood, simple language and should provide the participants with an adequate rationale for the meeting he or she is about to "go to."

*Role Descriptions*

During each session, each participant takes on a role which is described in an individual booklet or rolecard. Since most Rolemaps involve five participants, each session must have five different roles. (For greater flexibility, an optional sixth role is often included in the Rolemap design.)

*Choosing roles.* Just as with sessions, roles must represent some reasonable reality. The job titles or other titles used must reflect the roles of people who hold decision-making or otherwise significant positions or opinions with regard to the issue under consideration. For example, in *Screaming Committees* (concerned with the general issue of the selection of instructional materials in the schools), the titles assigned to the various roles for the two sessions include the following:

| SESSION I | SESSION II |
|---|---|
| • *Director of Curriculum* | • *Superintendent of Schools* |
| • *Principal, Washington Middle School* | • *Parent, Community Action Group* |
| • *Teacher, Monroe Elementary School* | • *Parent, Biochemist* |
| • *Teacher, Adams High School* | • *Minister* |
| • *Parent* | • *Publishers' Representative* |

In addition to representing significant people in the real world, the grouping of roles within a session must also reflect reality. For example, all of the roles which exist together within each of the two sessions above might reasonably come together at a meeting in the real world.

*Balancing roles within a session.* In each session, roles should be constructed to maintain a balance. The simplest balance within a session can be achieved by assigning an even number of roles to opposite viewpoints. For example, in Session II of *Screaming Committees,* two people are strongly opposed to the adoption of a particular science series, while two others are strongly supportive of this series. (See Figure

2.) More realistic (and more time-consuming to achieve in design) is a balance achieved through subtler means, e.g., with multiple (rather than two) perspectives, with positions held in common but for quite different reasons, with different priorities assigned to the same positions, and so forth. The careful balancing of roles through such complex considerations not only better reflects most real-world realities, but also better facilitates rich discussion—rather than the "one side versus the other" kind.

*Facilitating discussion.* In most Rolemaps, one role in each session is that of a neutral facilitator, who is instructed to remain neutral and to facilitate discussion among the other role players. For example, in Session II of *Screaming Committees,* F. Powers, the Superintendent of the Lincoln County School District, is designated the neutral facilitator and, after a brief role description, these instructions are provided:

---

### *HOW DO YOU BEGIN?*

---

- *Introduce yourself and indicate the purpose of the meeting, i.e., to discuss the science series and share feelings and opinions.*
- *Ask others to introduce themselves.*
- *Intervene in case of arguments.*
- *Be sure everyone gets to talk.*

---

Among the specific functions assigned to such a neutral role may be the following:
- keep participants on task;
- don't allow discussion to bog down on trivial points;
- avoid specific problems identified by the designer;
- encourage shy people to talk;
- break off those who would monopolize discussion;
- ask leading questions;
- look for "implicit assumptions" to probe gently; and
- summarize.

*Figure 2*

*Positive and Negative Roles*
*(from **Screaming Committees**, Session II)*

---

**OPPOSED TO ADOPTION**
**S. Shuster (Parent, Community Action Group)**

You have four children, and you recently moved into Lincoln County. You make a decent home for your family, just as your parents did before you. And, you try to teach your children about right and wrong.

The new science series is about the worst thing you've ever seen. To start with, the books are just plain smutty. No child should be looking at pictures like the ones in these books. And if that wasn't bad enough, the books don't really teach anything. Instead of presenting facts to be learned, they just raise questions, send students off to learn on their own, and challenge what is known. Kids don't need books to help them do this.

And, some of the assignments actually ask boys to cook at home in their kitchen. What are they trying to make boys into? And, the pictures! Some show girls doing men's jobs, and most of them are of foreigners. Whatever happened to plain, ordinary Americans? After all, America has the best scientists in the world.

**D. Russell (Minister)**

You are a highly respected minister who is often invited to speak in the East End. One of the major topics of interest to you and to your listeners has been "The Education of Our Children in Today's Schools." As a part of your presentation for a speech recently, you decided to glance through some textbooks which are used in the local schools. While one of the youth groups met after school in your church, you borrowed some of the students' books and skimmed them. Boy, did you ever get a shock!

The new science series is just about as disgusting as textbooks can get. Evolution is taught as a fact, and not just as one of a number of theories. On top of that, the books are loaded with anti-U.S. propaganda. Communists are often portrayed as scientific heroes while our own scientists are neglected. The books you

---

*(Continued on Next Page)*

*Figure 2 (Continued)*

sampled didn't have human reproduction as a topic, but you understand that some of the parents in your church are upset about other books in the series because of the graphic pictures of sex organs.

---

**SUPPORTIVE OF ADOPTION**
**V. Pappas (Parent, Biochemist)**

As a biochemist you believe that science is far more than facts and figures. It's learning and applying the scientific method—making hypotheses, gathering data, drawing reasonable conclusions. It's a powerful approach to understanding our world and to solving some of our world's problems.

Because of all the recent excitement in the newspapers, you recently looked at your child's science book. Were you ever surprised! It was the most interesting, well-written textbook you've ever seen. You wish they'd had books like that when you were a student. The prose was clear and easy to read. It related to ordinary things in the real community. The experiments were well-designed and relevant to the content. And, when you asked some students for an opinion, you found that most of the better students think it's the greatest science course they've had so far. Boys and girls alike have enjoyed the scientific approach to cooking, gardening, and transmitting messages. Anything that can turn kids on to science the way this series seems to be doing should be used as a model for other textbooks.

**B. Taylor (Publishers' Representative)**

You're a salesman for a publishing house, but you're also an ex-principal and an ex-science teacher. The publishers picked you to attend this meeting because they know you to be level-headed and good at getting people to see perspectives other than their own.

You believe that Cogent Publishers responsibly serves the schools, emphasizing quality education more than any other textbook publisher you know. You have a number of background facts about this particular series which you hope to present during the meeting:

*(Continued on Next Page)*

## *Figure 2 (Continued)*

- The series, *EVERYONE A SCIENTIST,* was developed by a panel of outstanding scientists and educators.
- The series was field-tested with learners all over the nation and revised on the basis of these trials.
- Representatives from federal bureaus and national organizations were consulted to eliminate all ethnic, political, social, religious, and sexual biases.
- The series is reasonably priced.
- Sales have been spectacular and consumer reviews highly favorable.

Such a role must also be appropriate to the role-character to which it is assigned. For example, neutrality is commonly associated with a position of power (e.g., vice president, superintendent of schools, etc.) or with the role of an objective outsider (newspaper reporter, consultant, etc.). As the sessions change, a different participant is assigned to the neutral role. This is done for two reasons: (a) people vary in their ability as facilitators and a very poor one could mar the entire Rolemap if left in that role throughout, and (b) playing the facilitator is generally not so interesting as playing the other roles.

### Role-Playing Sessions

A session is a period of time (usually between eight and 15 minutes) in which the participants in a small group take on appointed roles and hold a discussion around selected aspects of a central topic. The reason for the meeting may itself be the basis for controversy (e.g., the meeting has been called to discuss community complaints about a science series selected for adoption), or the focus may be less situation-bound (e.g., a group of people get into a discussion about management systems in the company cafeteria). The "people" brought together in a session must, as indicated earlier, seem appropriate to be together. A single Rolemap usually has from two to four sessions which are represented as meetings—either formal or informal. These sessions occur in chronological order, although the time passed in between sessions may vary from a few minutes to years.

*Maintaining instructional control.* Sessions—and their introductory set-ups—are so designed that the flow of Rolemap action is independent of anything said, done, or decided within a session. The emphasis in sessions is always on discussion and not on decision-making. However, the content of the set-ups and the role descriptions is such that, even if a decision were made during a session, it would not impact on subsequent set-ups or sessions. For example, the focus in Session I of *Screaming Committees* is on sources of information which should be considered in selecting textbooks. Roles are so described that discussion is indicated. However, even if the participants somehow took a vote and decided on specific information sources to be used in selecting textbooks, such a decision would have no impact on the content of the set-up which follows Session I and introduces Session II, the content of which is summarized as follows:

*It is one year after your first role-play session. Let me share with you what's happened in the past year. Dr. Sanford's selection committee continued to meet for several months and finally chose a science series called EVERYONE A SCIENTIST. A few months ago, the teachers got their desk copies and everyone seemed satisfied. Then, about two weeks ago, shortly after the new books began to be used in the classrooms, the parents of a third grader registered a complaint. Stirred up by these parents, other parents began to look into the series and organized a Community Action Group to get rid of the books. However, the local newspaper published an editorial about this time in support of the books. This is where Session II begins.*

*Superintendent Powers has called a meeting in his office to discuss the issue of the science series. Others at the meeting are Shuster, a parent who represents the Community Action Group; Russell, a minister from one of the local churches; Pappas, a professional scientist as well as a parent; and Taylor, who represents the publishing house which produced the science series.*

*One of you is Superintendent Powers who will facilitate the meeting. Two are the parents, Shuster and Pappas, one is Minister Russell, and the last is the publishers' representative, Taylor.*

*Please set your card up. It should say Session II. Read your role carefully and, when Superintendent Powers calls the*

*meeting to order, be prepared to introduce yourself. Have a
good session.*

Clearly, it makes no difference what decisions were made
about information sources in Session I. The situation
presented to set up Session II is independent—and deliberately designed to be so. Hence, procedural and instructional
controls remain in the hands of the Rolemap designer.

*Action-facilitating events.* Control is increased and the
action of a Rolemap is moved forward by periodically
introducing information about critical events. Such critical
events can occur at any time in the Rolemap. However, most
commonly, such critical information is introduced during the
set-ups to a session. During the set-up, the narrator may, for
example, say: "A parents' group has brought suit and . . ." or
"The President of the Caduceus Corporation just mandated
that . . ." or "A new federal law was passed which . . ." Such
pronouncements—based always on believable realities—
further the action and are beyond question by the participants. However, such events may be announced during
sessions. They may take the form of a memorandum, letter,
or news item which the audiotape narrator announces, or the
neutral facilitator or one of the players finds in his or her role
booklet with instructions. The critical information introduced must be *logically independent* of anything that
participants may say, do, or decide within their discussion
sessions, and the source of such information must be credible
to the other players and the announcement taken as an
absolute.

### Closing Comments

Closing comments are just what their name implies. They
are the narrator's words which indicate to the participants
that the role plays have come to an end. "Back to the real
world." Such comments should be short and sweet, as
illustrated in these from *Screaming Committees*:

*Well, that was quite a meeting. It's time to relax a bit, end your role playing, and come back to the real world.*

*In this simulation, we attempted to portray some of the problems involved in the selection of curriculum materials. Let's take a few minutes now to debrief; to share some of your feelings and thoughts as you played out your roles in the simulated meetings. Workshop Leader? Would you help us debrief?*

### Debriefing

The importance of the debriefing period in achieving the objectives of the Rolemap varies, dependent upon the instructional objectives and the context in which the Rolemap is used. If, for example, the Rolemap is used primarily as a motivational activity intended to get people involved in the general topic and in a mode of active learning, then little more may be required than the facilitation of spontaneous comments about feelings and ideas. The assumption, in this case, is that other instructional activities or materials will carry the heavier instructional burden.

However, in the more common case in which a Rolemap is used not only to motivate, but also to meet both affective and cognitive objectives related to the central issue, debriefing has a critical role. After an initial period of more-or-less spontaneous catharsis (during which anyone can say anything without judgment or analysis), the workshop leader follows a carefully worked-out list of topics and questions designed to cover the instructional objectives stated prior to Rolemap design. These objectives were the basis for determining the specific sessions themselves and for the content of the set-ups and role descriptions. In *Screaming Committees,* such questions included the following:

- *The first session was one which occurred prior to adoption of a textbook series; the second was not only after adoption was completed but after a*

*community complaint had been lodged. What affec-
tive differences did you notice between the two
sessions? Do you think this relates to what happens in
the real world?*

- *For those of you who played the role of opposing the
adoption, that is, the roles of S. Shuster and D.
Russell, how did you feel in those roles? (If people
report special enjoyment in playing these roles, ask
them why they think they enjoyed them so.)*

- *For those of you who played the role of supporting
the adoption, that is, the roles of V. Pappas and B.
Taylor, how did you feel in those roles? (If people
report special frustration in playing these roles, ask
them why they felt frustrated.)*

- *How do you feel the "complaint" session compared
with real-world events?*

- *How do you think such confrontations could be
avoided?*

These questions were designed to match only a few of the
instructional objectives for *Screaming Committees.*

### The Relationship Between the Elements
### and the Content of a Rolemap

Regardless of how attractive the elements of a Rolemap
appear to be, the instructional effectiveness of the activity
depends upon the content presented.

#### *The Central Issue*

For a Rolemap to exist, there should be a central and
controversial issue—a problem, a question, a task—which
provides the *raison d'etre* and ties the entire activity together.
Issues which have provided the content for various Rolemaps
include the following:

- the integration of handicapped children into the
regular classroom (mainstreaming);

- small-group techniques for management training;
- simulations and games for college instruction;
- implementation of corporate management systems in branch hospitals; and
- selection of instructional materials for schools.

Obviously, the issue chosen should be relevant and significant to the participants. For example, the Rolemap *Screaming Committees*—which deals with the broad issue of the selection of instructional materials—was designed as one part of a larger, packaged workshop for school personnel who have been or will be involved in the selection process. Obviously, the issue is relevant and important to those participants.

The appropriateness of a central issue can also be usefully described by indicating what kinds of issues are *not* appropriate. For example, topics which are *not* appropriate include the following:

- those about which the issues are very simple and clear-cut;
- those about which there "really" is only one reasonable point of view;
- those about which very little is known;
- those about which the participants know very little; or
- those about which the participants are involved in such a way that a Rolemap might be offensive or distressing.

### Sub-Issues

An analysis of the central issue should reveal controversial sub-issues and reflect various associated opinions and attitudes. For example, an initial list of sub-issues related to the selection of textbooks includes the following:

- *What sources of information should be used in selection?*
- *How can information sources be relied upon?*

- *What problems occur in trying to meet the needs of the community in the selection of textbooks?*
- *What can be done when people disagree?*
- *How can sufficient time be allowed for truly adequate selection?*
- *What selection procedures or system should be used?*
- *What selection criteria should be used?*
- *What documentation of selection procedures should be made and kept?*
- *Who should select?*
- *Who should have the final word on selection?*
- *How often should basic series be selected?*

Two sub-issues were ultimately chosen from this list to get the lion's share of attention in the Rolemap:

- *What sources of information should be used in selection?*
- *What problems occur in trying to meet the needs of the community in the selection of textbooks?*

The first issue provided the basis for Session I, characterized as "the first, formal meeting of a selection committee made up of school personnel and a parent to discuss the information sources deemed important." The second issue provided the basis for Session II, characterized as "a meeting of school and non-school personnel (including some angry parents) after a strong complaint by a citizens' group has been made against a science series already adopted."

Note that one way of "setting up" a session is through the introduction of a critical event that requires a response of some sort. Thus, in the example above, the issue of "What problems occur in trying to meet the needs of the community in the selection of textbooks?" was introduced by a "critical event," namely, the protest of a group of angry parents. The issue involved in this session could have been discussed within the context of a meeting, e.g., called by the school district to get initial inputs from various citizens' groups. However, the Rolemap designers felt that such a meeting would not only be unrealistic, but might fail to elicit the kinds of responses to which they wanted workshop participants to be exposed.

*Role-Models (or Significant People in the Real World)*

In addition to sub-issues, a Rolemap requires that you represent in the roles those people in the real world who hold significant views toward those sub-issues. In *Screaming Committees,* the sub-issue of Session I was concerned with what information sources should be used in selecting text-books. Hence, the list of people whose opinions, perspectives, and decisions might be important and, hence, who might serve as role-models for the Rolemap roles, included the following: teachers, principals, curriculum coordinators, li-brarians, superintendents, content specialists, parents, other citizens, publishers' representatives, and consultants. And, the roles actually chosen for Session I included the following:

- *director of curriculum;*
- *principal;*
- *two teachers; and*
- *parent.*

Specific procedures for developing roles, as well as the other Rolemap elements, are given in detail in Chapter V.

# IV.

## OUTCOMES

The outcomes for the participants in a Rolemap, at minimum, will be heightened interest and involvement in the instructional situation. So long as the topic is appropriately chosen and the mechanics of Rolemap design and implementation are effectively executed, the opportunity to engage in active discussion within a non-threatening format and with others of like interests seems to be a highly motivating and satisfying experience for workshop participants. In a long workshop or series of classroom meetings, the Rolemap represents a welcome break in the use of lecture or other instructional modes.

However, the Rolemap can do more than interest and activate participants. It can also provide an instructionally appropriate and effective means of presenting one type of information—namely, information about the major aspects and multiple viewpoints associated with a controversial issue of importance to the instructional domain and to the participants. Furthermore, the Rolemap can do this in a dynamic way that simulates the complex realities of the controversial issue as it exists in the real world. Subsequent debriefing not only can emphasize and clarify these realities but also can lead to group problem-solving and action directed toward coping with the controversy.

From the trainer or designer's standpoint, this design

offers just one more tool for instructional development. And—like the child with a hammer—*having* a tool leads to *use* of it. For example, one trainer/designer has—in the past two years—developed six Rolemaps for use in a variety of training settings, e.g., public schools, governmental agencies, and industry. The history of a Rolemap design series at Indiana University will illustrate the point well. In 1973, at one of Indiana's centers, a Rolemap was developed. Based upon a preview of that Rolemap, in 1976, staff at another Indiana center designed a second Rolemap. Then, in 1978, this second Rolemap was modified to fit a slightly different target population. Since that time, this same staff has developed four additional Rolemaps for other purposes. (All of these are listed under Resources, Chapter VI.)

Rolemap design seems to lend itself to adaptation and new design ideas. One of the Rolemaps mentioned above, through several design iterations, ended up as a combination of a Rolemap and a simulation game. Another Rolemap led one workshop participant to a solution for his training problem. He had the need to provide (in less than two hours) new teachers with training in parent conference techniques. While he saw the advantages of role playing in this training situation, he was concerned that such unstructured activities would get out of control—both timewise and instructionally. After experiencing a Rolemap himself, he decided that printed, structured role descriptions would be an effective way to get new teachers to role play (in pairs) a teacher-parent conference for subsequent small-group feedback.

Familiarity with the design of a Rolemap—just as with other instructional designs, e.g., film or the sound-slide set—does lead to repeated use and adaptation. Like any other solution, though, one must guard against applying it to all problems, regardless of the fit. However, in an instructional situation in which a controversial issue exists for study, and role playing seems appropriate but too unpredictable, a

Rolemap may be the answer—preserving the strengths of role plays while eliminating the potential weaknesses.

# V.

# DEVELOPMENTAL GUIDE

This chapter assumes that you have a learner population in mind and that you have selected a Rolemap as the appropriate instructional design* for dealing with a controversial issue of concern to that population.

For example, one Rolemap—*Playing Your Way Through School*—was designed for participants who were faculty members from a foreign university. They had been selected by their dean and sent to a workshop to "learn everything about simulations and games" and then return home to disseminate the ideas throughout the faculty. The broad instructional goals for the workshop were two: (1) to know all they could about simulations and games, and (2) to know how to effectively introduce S/G to their university faculty. Most of the one-week workshop was addressed to the first goal; however, it was decided that a Rolemap (in conjunction with a lecture and readings on the adoption of innovations) would be an appropriate technique for meeting part of the second goal. The broad goals are indicated in Figure 3, with the dashed-line box indicating the domain of Rolemap responsi-

---

*Before attempting to develop a Rolemap, you may find it useful to have participated in or led one yourself. So that this will be possible, a complete Rolemap, *Playing Your Way Through School,* is provided in Appendix B, along with instructions for a simple tryout.

*Figure 3*

*Instructional Goals Associated with a
One-Week Workshop on Simulations and Games*

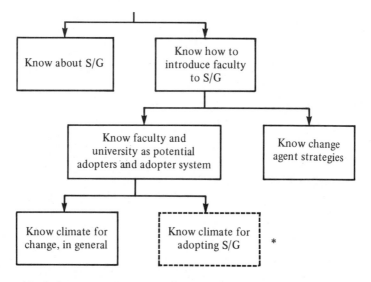

*Dashed-line box indicates use of Rolemap to meet instructional goal.

bility. It should be recalled that a Rolemap is appropriate to an instructional goal which involves knowing about and understanding various viewpoints and rationales regarding a controversial issue. In this example, the goal being addressed by the Rolemap was "know the climate in your university for accepting and adopting S/G as instructional techniques." The controversial issue involved was "the use of S/G in university instruction."

This chapter offers a guide to the step-by-step development of a Rolemap. The development steps fall into three phases: pre-design, design, and production activities. These three phases and their detailed steps are listed in Figure 4 and elaborated on in the rest of this chapter. Although the steps

*Figure 4*

*Steps in Development*

---

**Pre-Design Activities**

    1. Analyze controversial issue into sub-issues.

    2. Identify significant role-models.

    3. Compare with participants' entry level.

    4. Select sub-issues and state instructional objectives as debriefing questions.

**Design Activities**

    1. Specify sessions.

    2. Specify roles.

    3. Fill in design matrix.

    4. Write script and role descriptions.

    5. Rewrite debriefing questions.

    6. Prepare and debug prototype on convenient audience.

    7. Try out on representatives of target population.

**Production Activities**

    1. Prepare final audiotape.

    2. Prepare final role description booklets or cards and role labels.

    3. Prepare leader's guide.

---

are presented here sequentially, in practice some are more iterative than sequential.

### Pre-Design Activities

Pre-design activities include analyzing the controversial issue, identifying the significant role-models, making comparisons with the participants' entry level, and stating the instructional objectives as debriefing questions (see Figure 5). First, the controversial issue should be analyzed into sub-issues and significant role-models associated with the sub-issues. The results of this analysis, when compared with the participants' entry level, provide the basis for the instructional objectives of the Rolemap and for their direct implementation in the Rolemap itself.

1. *Analyze controversial issue into sub-issues.* The controversial issue can be analyzed into sub-issues by asking (yourself and others with experience and expertise) such questions as:

- What are the major areas of concern regarding this issue?
- What aspects of the issue cause controversy?

For example, in *Playing Your Way Through School,* the controversial issue is the use of simulations and games in university instruction. Among the sub-issues or areas of concern identified in the analysis phase were the following:

- experience of instructor;
- suitability for different subject areas;
- utilization time;
- appropriateness for adult learners;
- non-traditional format;
- capabilities for meeting instructional objectives;
- motivational capabilities; and
- preparation time.

Once sub-issues were identified, each was examined for *opinions and attitudes* associated with it. For example,

*Figure 5*

*Pre-Design Activities*

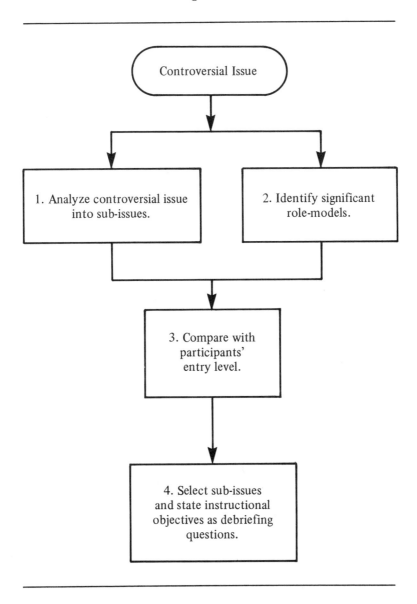

"preparation time" was viewed by some as heavy and quite unreasonable given other instructional demands, while others felt that no more was involved than "reading the instructions." Regarding "experience of instructor," some felt that only an instructor with a great deal of experience with S/G should try to use them in the classroom; others felt that experience was less necessary than an open mind with regard to instructional techniques. Also, some people held opinions very strongly; others had only mild opinions. And so it went.

The analysis of the controversial issue should result in a list of sub-issues or concerns, accompanied by the kinds of opinions and attitudes which are importantly associated with them in the real world.

2. *Identify significant role-models.* Just as with sub-issues, role-models provide a basis for stating the instructional objectives and for implementing them in the Rolemap. And, once sub-issues and associated opinions and attitudes have been stated, role-models are relatively easy to identify. Such questions as the following can help:

- What classes of people hold strong opinions about these sub-issues?
- What classes of people are importantly affected by these sub-issues?

Try to include people with a variety of perspectives, e.g., people who are both decision-makers and those acted-upon, people who are both liberal and conservative, people who are both goal- and people-oriented, people who are both positive and negative, people who are both simplistic and complex in perspective, people who are both emotional and rational, people who are both innovative and foot-dragging, people who have both short- and long-term views, and so forth.

For example, in the analysis phase of developing *Playing Your Way Through School,* four classes of people or role-models were identified: (1) faculty from various departments, (2) administrators, (3) students, and (4) parents.

3. *Compare with participants' entry level.* Before moving from issue analysis to actual Rolemap design, compare the results of the analysis—the sub-issues or concerns, significant role-models, and opinions and attitudes held—with the participants' entry level.

- Do the participants know enough about the sub-issues to engage in meaningful discussion?
- Which sub-issues are likely to be most important and most relevant to the participants?
- Which classes of people (role-models) should the participants know about?
- What opinions and attitudes do your participants most need to be aware of and understand?

For example, in *Playing Your Way Through School,* the participants had some information about S/G from earlier reading, but they were not really widely experienced or knowledgeable. However, they were going home as "experts," and they would face a lot of questions and challenges with their "new" techniques. The Rolemap would provide them with some information and experience regarding the nature and sources of questions, complaints, and problems. And— while they brought limited information regarding S/G to the Rolemap—they knew well the university environment they came from, and, hence, would be able to enrich the roles they would play.

4. *Select sub-issues and state instructional objectives as debriefing questions.* Once the central, controversial issue has been analyzed into sub-issues, associated opinions and attitudes, and role-models, and these have been compared with the entry level and needs of the participants, the sub-issues of greatest importance and relevance to the participants can be selected and converted into instructional objectives.

For example, in *Playing Your Way Through School,* it was decided that the three most important sub-issues were:

(1) suitability for different subject areas;

(2) appropriateness for adult learners; and

(3) capabilities for meeting instructional objectives;

and these three were converted into the following instructional objectives:

> (1) be aware of faculty needs, particularly with regard to the selection of S/G for different subject areas;
>
> (2) know common criticisms and relevant track-record for S/G with adult learners; and
>
> (3) know the strengths and weaknesses of S/G for instructional use.

After stating the instructional objectives, and before developing the Rolemap itself, it is useful to make at least a rough draft of the content-related (not catharsis-related) debriefing questions. Questions at this early stage of development may take a very general form, e.g., "What differences did you see in attitude toward S/G among faculty members from different academic disciplines?" After the Rolemap is completed, this question may become much more specific to the roles played and take such a form as "H. Kent and J. Rodriguez were both positive toward S/G, while M. Boyd and G. Navarro were both negative. Can you draw any relationships between their attitudes and their academic disciplines?"

Also useful to state (and hence keep in mind throughout development) are those instructional objectives related to future applications.

- What subject areas "back home" do you expect to have trouble with?
- Who on the faculty do you think may object to S/G for adult learners?
- How can you demonstrate that S/G can meet specific instructional objectives?

**Design Activities**

Based on sub-issues, role-models, and debriefing questions (instructional objectives), design activities include specification of the Rolemap sessions and roles, filling in the design matrix, writing the script and role descriptions, rewriting the debriefing questions, preparing and debugging a rough proto-type Rolemap, and—if possible—trying out the Rolemap on representatives from the target population (see Figure 6). Again, note the iterative nature of the first two steps, as indicated by their parallel placement on the flowchart.

1. *Specify sessions.* Rolemap sessions are generally dis-crete meetings where participants discuss aspects of the central, controversial issue from their various role perspec-tives. These sessions focus on one or more of the selected sub-issues. For example, in *Playing Your Way Through School,* Session I focuses primarily on the sub-issue of "suitability for different subject areas," as is reflected in the description of the session (see Figure 7) and the meeting of various academic department chairpersons. Session II focuses primarily on "appropriateness for adult learners," and Session III focuses primarily on "capabilities for meeting instructional objectives." However, all three sessions include some reference to sub-issues other than the one of primary focus, even including some of the issues not chosen as the three most important.

Once you have decided what sub-issues should be empha-sized, you must design an appropriate "meeting." A question to ask is "*Why* and *where* might a meeting occur in which significant people would get together to discuss the issues selected?" In *Playing Your Way Through School,* the first and the third sessions involve formal meetings called by university administrators. The second session is an informal meeting, characterized as a group interview by a campus newspaper reporter.

2. *Specify roles.* Keeping the selected sub-issues in mind, ask "Who are the significant people (or role-models identified earlier) who might reasonably come together to discuss the sub-issue(s)?" If you have a number of sub-issues to cover in

*Figure 6*

*Design Activities*

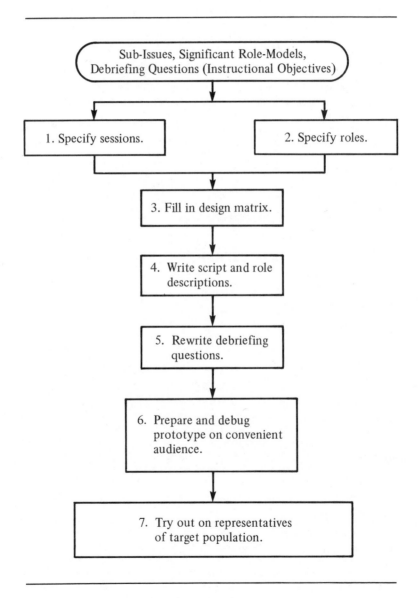

*Figure 7*

*Descriptions of Sessions*
*(from **Playing Your Way Through School**)*

---

**SESSION I**: The Coordinator of the Learning Resources Center at the university has just returned from a workshop on simulations and games and has invited the chairpersons of various academic departments to meet to discuss the strengths and weaknesses of S/G and their possible use in each of the departments.

**SESSION II**: After a month of faculty tryouts of S/G (as a result of an administrative memo), the students have been talking so much that the campus newspaper has sent its star reporter to interview some students about their own preferences about the use of S/G in general, and in specific classes.

**SESSION III**: After the appearance of a newspaper article on S/G, which quoted some faculty and students out of context, there have been public complaints and the Academic Vice President has called a meeting of faculty and student representatives to discuss how well S/G are meeting specific instructional objectives. That is, "Are the students really learning anything using S/G?"

---

one session, you may want to list them one-by-one with relevant role-models beside each.

Eventually, you must choose five (or six, if an optional role is included) roles for each session or "meeting." For example, in *Playing Your Way Through School* the following roles were chosen:

SESSION I:    **Administrator: Coordinator of Learning Resources Center**

Faculty: *Chairperson of Language Department*

Faculty: *Chairperson of Mathematics Department*

Faculty: *Chairperson of Political Science Department*

Faculty: *Chairperson of Business Department*

SESSION II:    **Student: reporter, university newspaper**

Student: *student in economics class*

Student: *student in business class*

Student: *student in mathematics class*

Student: *student in political science class*

SESSION III: **Administrator: Vice President of Academic Affairs**

Administrator: *Coordinator of Learning Resources Center*

Faculty: *Chairperson of Mathematics Department*

Student: *representative of Student Union*

Student: *representative of Student Union*

Note that one of the five roles developed will be the neutral facilitator in each session. This role must be compatible with the function of facilitating a meeting, e.g., an authority figure or a neutral outsider. In Session I of *Playing*

*Your Way Through School,* the facilitator's role is that of the Coordinator of the Learning Resources Center, an administrative job which is slightly outside of the mainstream of the regular faculty departments. In Session II, the facilitator's role is that of a campus newspaper reporter, a student role somewhat separated from the other student roles. In Session III, the facilitator's role is that of the Vice President of Academic Affairs, clearly an authority figure.

The four other roles should be compatible with that of the neutral facilitator, i.e., they must be reasonable together. However, it is even more important that the other four be balanced across perspectives. This can be most simply achieved by having two people on one side and two on the other. For example, in Session I of *Playing Your Way Through School,* two chairpersons are supportive of S/G and two are opposed to S/G. However, since such simple positions neither reflect reality nor generate interesting discussion, these roles are more complex in design than at first they appear. Figure 8 includes the role descriptions for J. Rodriguez and H. Kent, both of whom are positive toward simulations and games, but for different reasons and to a different degree.

3. *Fill in design matrix.* At this point in the development of a Rolemap, it is important to keep track of the various roles and their valences (zero, plus, minus) with regard to different sessions and to different issues. This can become a complex process when numerous controversial issues are counterbalanced across four or more roles. Just one issue counterbalanced across four roles is complex enough. However, even a relatively simple situation (e.g., two positive and two negative roles), which changes from session to session, can be difficult to follow. The use of a design matrix is suggested.

Figure 9 illustrates a design matrix with valences filled in. Sessions are indicated across the top and players (participants) down the left. Valences are shown in the cells. In most cases, valences can be entered before any detail is added to the design matrix—beyond specification of number of sessions and roles. The neutral facilitator's role (indicated by a zero) is distributed diagonally, beginning with Player A, Session I and continuing through Player C, Session III. In this way, the neutral facilitator's role will be assigned to three different players or participants. Next, the pluses and minuses are distributed so that each player and each session will get a balance of roles. So long as both rows and columns are checked, balance should be achieved.

The design matrix for *Playing Your Way Through School* (see Figure 10) indicates that in Session I, two players are positive toward the use of simulations and games in a university and two players are negative toward their use. However, as seen in Figure 8, these "pure" positions are implemented through role descriptions which make them quite different.

4. *Write script and role descriptions.* Writing the script (introduction, session set-ups, and closing comments) and writing the role descriptions (which amounts to 15 role descriptions in a Rolemap of three sessions with five roles each) is likely to be an iterative activity, and one which takes place over a fairly extended period of time. While an outline or rough draft of a script may be written first, it will need revision after the characterizations of the roles have been developed. By the same token, after the final script is written, roles will probably need to be revised. All in all, it would be a mistake to think that a final script or final role descriptions can be written independently. The following three-step procedure may be helpful:

- *Outline.* Make a detailed outline of the script. This should cover not only the introduction, session set-ups, and closing comments, but also any critical events used to heighten interest and further the

*Figure 8*

*Two Positive Roles for Comparison*
*(from **Playing Your Way Through School**, Session I)*

---

J. RODRIGUEZ
Chairperson
Language Department
Globe University

You are new to the faculty at Globe. You have had five years of successful teaching at a very progressive and expensive college.

You like to try out new things. In fact, your application and development of new instructional techniques in your own field is part of why you got this job. But, you realize that more traditional faculty members do not always like your innovativeness, and Globe has a reputation for being old-fashioned. However, through establishing good relations with the administration and the chairpersons, you hope to have an impact on the university's teaching techniques.

You skimmed the Simulations/Games Workshop Manual which the LRC Coordinator sent to you and you find some of the ideas quite relevant to your field. Specifically, you can see using S/G to accomplish such basic goals as improving vocabulary and spelling or such high-level goals as teaching citizens the skills necessary to affect what their newspapers print. You are ready to try S/G in your classrooms.

---

H. KENT
Chairperson
Political Science Department
Globe University

You are the head of the Political Science Department at Globe University. You are a relatively independent person, but one who

*(Continued on Next Page)*

*Figure 8 (Continued)*

takes others' opinions and needs into account. You have a secure position in your field and in this university, and you like both the teaching and the administrative ends of your job.

You had been a bit curious about what simulations and games might have to offer the Political Science Department since you heard a little about them at the last annual convention you attended. However, after trying to wade through that 400-page manual of instructional simulations and games which the LRC Coordinator gave you, you are not so sure. There seems to be a lot involved just in learning how to find and use materials which are already developed. And you had been interested in developing some things of your own, but unless they will give you the semester off, that doesn't seem possible. You are overwhelmed and discouraged.

*Figure 9*

*A Design Matrix*

|  | SESSION I | SESSION II | SESSION III |
|---|---|---|---|
| PLAYER A | O | + | — |
| PLAYER B | — | O | + |
| PLAYER C | + | — | O |
| PLAYER D | — | + | — |
| PLAYER E | + | — | + |

*Figure 10*

## The Design Matrix for *Playing Your Way Through School*

| | SESSION I | SESSION II | SESSION III |
|---|---|---|---|
| **PLAYER A** | ◯<br><br>J. Sanford<br><br>Coordinator,<br>LRC | —<br><br>A. Smith<br><br>Student,<br>Economics | ✛<br><br>R. Reston<br><br>Representative,<br>Student Union |
| **PLAYER B** | ✛<br><br>J. Rodriguez<br><br>Chairperson,<br>Language Dept. | ◯<br><br>M. McCullough<br><br>Reporter,<br>*Globe U.*<br>*Gazette* | —<br><br>V. Pappas<br><br>Representative,<br>Student Union |
| **PLAYER C** | —<br><br>G. Navarro<br><br>Chairperson,<br>Mathematics<br>Dept. | ✛<br><br>C. Mason<br><br>Student,<br>Business | ◯<br><br>M. Tracy<br><br>Vice President,<br>Academic<br>Affairs |
| **PLAYER D** | ✛<br><br>H. Kent<br><br>Chairperson,<br>Political Sci.<br>Dept. | —<br><br>D. Russell<br><br>Student,<br>Mathematics | ✛<br><br>J. Sanford<br><br>Coordinator,<br>LRC |
| **PLAYER E** | —<br><br>M. Boyd<br><br>Chairperson,<br>Business Dept. | ✛<br><br>F. Powers<br><br>Student,<br>Political<br>Science | —<br><br>G. Navarro<br><br>Chairperson,<br>Mathematics<br>Dept. |

action. Once the outline of the script is completed, descriptions of the role characterizations should be developed. These can be as simple as a list of phrases describing each character.

- *Write.* You may find it useful to write the script and the role descriptions in the order in which they will occur in the completed Rolemap activity (i.e., introduction, Session I set-up, Session I role descriptions, Session II set-up, Session II role descriptions, and so forth through the closing comments).
- *Edit and review.* After a break of at least several days, read the script and the role descriptions—still in the order in which they will occur in the Rolemap. Edit for continuity as well as for grammatical and typographical errors. Revise as necessary.

a. *The script.* The script provides the continuity for the entire Rolemap activity. It introduces the Rolemap, provides set-ups for the sessions, interjects critical events or information to further the action, and indicates when the role-playing activity is over.

In the introduction, there is probably no need to mention the word "Rolemap" or even the title of a particular Rolemap. Both of these bits of information may be of interest to the instructional developer or, if the Rolemap is disseminated or marketed, to potential users/purchasers. However, from the participants' standpoint, they may be distractors. Participants do need to know what the central topic is, how they should group themselves, what to expect in the way of audiotape or other instructions, and what they themselves will be doing (e.g., reading an individual booklet and playing roles in a simulated discussion group).

The introductory comments for *Playing Your Way Through School* went this way:

*Hello. Welcome to this workshop event. I'm going to be your guide through a series of discussions on the topic of simulations and games for university instruction.*

*In order to participate in this activity, you should be
seated in groups of five. Each group will engage in a series of
role-play activities. In each activity, you will take on a
different role. In a few minutes, you will receive a booklet
which will tell you **who to be** and **what to do**. But, first, let
me describe the situation in your first role-play activity . . .*

If the introduction is being handled by an audiotape
narrator, a news commentator approach is desirable. (An
understated Walter Cronkite will do nicely.) The introduction—as well as the other parts of the narration—should be
simple and unobtrusive. In general, attempts at humor
usually fail; however, with skillful handling and a sizeable
investment of both time and money, a dramatic treatment
can be quite effective. For example, in *Kenny* (see Appendix
A) the introduction and the initial set-up were originally
developed in sound-slide format and subsequently converted
into a sound filmstrip format. This was a nationally disseminated activity and, hence, the increased production costs
were appropriate. The script of this production and descriptions of the pictures appear in Appendix A.

The script of the audiotape narration also provides the
set-ups to each session. Through this means, the participants
are told where they are meeting and something about with
whom they are meeting. Also, critical information regarding
externally controlled events (e.g., a new law or regulation, a
news item, a crisis) is integrated into these set-ups. This sort
of information tends to heighten the participants' focus on
and interest in a session's discussion and to further the action
of the Rolemap as a whole.

The introduction of *Playing Your Way Through School*
blends into the set-up for Session I:

*As the story opens, we are in the office of the Coordinator
of the Learning Resources Center, J. Sanford. Sanford just
returned from a workshop on simulations and games and is
exploring the implementation of these techniques with the*

*faculty. Sanford has invited the chairpersons of faculty departments to a meeting to discuss these techniques.*

*Last week upon his return, he distributed copies of the Workshop Manual to each chairperson. His goal for this meeting is to hear from them what they think about S/G as instructional and cost-effective techniques for Globe University.*

*When you get your booklet, read the general role-play instructions on the first page. Then turn to Session I on the next page to see who you are. Read about yourself and set your booklet up so others can tell who you are. Okay, Coordinator Sanford, let's see what kind of a facilitator you are in getting your faculty to loosen up and discuss their real concerns and opinions about the implementation of simulations and games. You have ten minutes. Ready? Begin.*

The *closing comments* should be quite brief; they usually turn the workshop control over to the workshop leader.

*Well, have you had about enough of role playing for the time being? Okay, then, the time has come to look back at your experiences and share some of your feelings, concerns, or insights. I'll be leaving you now with your workshop leader. Goodbye from Globe University.*

Since the written script will be read aloud by a narrator, the developer/writer should try reading it aloud. It should read easily. Simple language, short sentences, and a flowing style help. Remember, you are writing spoken language, not textual material which can be re-read if not understood the first time. Also, although some redundancy is necessary, explanations about the activity should be kept to the minimum necessary for the participants to engage in the role-playing sessions. Don't tell them more than they need to know; you will only confuse them. Like other parts of the Rolemap, if you want to know if it works, try it out. To find out if the script is clear, read it to someone (a better test than having someone read it); to find out if continuity is maintained throughout the entire Rolemap, have a group go through it.

b. *Role descriptions.* The writer of role descriptions has the task of providing participants with enough information to play their roles (i.e., to present real-world arguments for and against, and to express real-world attitudes, biases, and opinions) and leaving enough unsaid so that participants can enrich the roles through their own knowledge and experience in the real world. Above all else, role descriptions should be cohesively informative about believable people. Role descriptions (with the help of the script) must account for both what the participants must know in order to play a role (e.g., something about simulations and games) and the justification within their roles for knowing it (e.g., having been given "a manual of Simulations and Games several days earlier by the Coordinator of the Learning Resources Center who called the meeting").

The potential developer of a Rolemap should be fore-warned that even for those who enjoy creative writing—narra-tion, dialogue, and characterization—the task of writing 15 role descriptions can be quite a burden. Writing just the five role descriptions required for a single session may take several hours. Therefore, it is suggested that this task be spaced over several days. However, it is also suggested that all role descriptions for a single session be detailed out, if not actually written, during one session. (Or, if this is not possible, it is suggested that any roles written be re-read before beginning to write others from the same session.) Since all roles in one session must "work" together, such an approach will tend to increase continuity and eliminate improbable combinations.

Also, in writing role descriptions, beware of writing to escape your own boredom, rather than to inform the role player. Generally, the first few role descriptions are rather interesting to write, but by the fourth or fifth, your enthusiasm is waning and, with ten left to do, there is a tendency for the writer to get a bit giddy, adding things for his or her own amusement (e.g., "cute" names, double meanings, etc.), or leaving things out because they have been said before (unfortunately, however, Player C will never read Player A's role description and, hence, what was said to Player A, if necessary for Player C, must be repeated).

Last, here are a few rules-of-thumb to use in writing role descriptions: (a) make each description less than one-third of a single-spaced page; (b) make all role descriptions in one session of the same length so that participants will finish reading at about the same time; and (c) write very simply—clear language, short sentences. Flowing prose is less important in role descriptions than clear, easily retrievable information. (Participants frequently look back during the discussion to check something in their role descriptions.)

5. *Rewrite debriefing questions.* Now that the sessions and role descriptions are designed and developed, debriefing questions can be made specific, e.g., a question can relate to specific roles played by a single player over several sessions, to the differences in interactions from one session to another, and so forth. Such questions can assist in meeting the instructional objectives—both affective and cognitive—of the Rolemap, as well as lead to real-world applications. However, debriefing should begin with a spontaneous sharing of feelings, i.e., with a period of catharsis.

a. *Catharsis.* Debriefing can begin with such open-ended questions as, "Would anyone like to share any feelings you had during the role plays?" If you have little experience in debriefing and have never asked this kind of question, you may feel like a bit of a fool the first time. However, if you follow two general rules for such debriefing, you will almost certainly survive, and the odds are even good that you will be both surprised and rewarded by the responses you will get. The two rules are these: (1) *be respectful* and (2) *be quiet.* If your tone of voice, your facial expression, your body language—indeed, if your entire attitude is one of respect for the participants and their views, no matter what those views are, they will tend to respond in kind, that is, to take your question seriously and to share some of their feelings and thoughts. In addition, you must realize that this kind of question requires serious thought; and people are not experienced at answering such questions. Therefore, as the question-asker, you must be able to tolerate silence—both theirs and yours. You must be able to wait for an answer. And, if—after a minute or so (oh, what a century it will seem)—no one says anything, you must be able to pass on to other questions without feeling like a failure as a leader or trying to make them feel like failures as participants. (After all, maybe no one had anything to share, or maybe no one wanted to share. That's okay.)

The purpose of this catharsis phase is primarily to get any pent-up emotions out in the open and out of the way so that the discussion can move on. However, after an initial period of unstructured sharing of feelings and thoughts, you can move to a more structured elicitation of feelings and thoughts relevant to certain roles or relationships among the roles.

For example, in *Playing Your Way Through School,* some of the more structured questions in the first phase of debriefing were these:

- *For those whose role characters held positions quite different from your own, how did you feel playing those parts?*
- *For those who were supposed to remain neutral and facilitate others in expressing opinions, how did you feel about your roles?*
- *For those who played the role of G. Navarro, who opposed the use of simulations and games in a university, how did you feel?*

Participants' responses to cathartic-type questions—unstructured and structured—will often lead them into the second phase of debriefing, i.e., an analysis of the content, particularly that aspect of the content which relates to different perspectives, different rationales, and different significant people.

b. *Instructional debriefing.* This phase involves both cognitive and affective domains and relates to the analysis of the issue of the Rolemap, its relevant controversial issues, the various perspectives which significant people have on the topic, and their rationales for those perspectives. The content of this phase of debriefing is largely determined by the issue analysis done prior to development of the Rolemap.

If time is limited, the leader may prefer to handle this phase of debriefing in a direct, pedagogical manner. For example, the leader may deliver a short lecture on the issue, a lecture designed to lay bare the structure of the content as determined during the analysis phase. If such an approach is taken, it would be well to allow time afterwards for participants to discuss the analysis—to disagree, to modify, to relate the Rolemap's analysis to their own experiences.

However, if time allows, a preferable and more demanding debriefing approach involves eliciting the issue analysis from the participants. If this approach is taken, a series of questions can be designed which—based on the developer's original issue analysis and on the instructional objectives—will guide the participants as they "re-discover" the controversial issues, varied perspectives and associated rationales, and significant people which make up the content of the Rolemap.

In *Playing Your Way Through School,* questions designed to elicit specific aspects of the content included the following:

- *In Session I, some people were positive and some were negative toward the use of simulations and games. Can you make any observations about the kinds of people who seemed to be positive?*

- *As a mathematics teacher with a heavy content load to cover, how did you feel about using simulations and games in your classroom?*

Questions can be designed to elicit both the cognitive and the affective aspects of the topic as it relates to the issue analysis underlying the Rolemap. Your instructional objectives, plus the lists of sub-issues, associated attitudes, and significant people, should provide you with a checklist for the design of debriefing activities.

c. *Real-world applications.* Even if there is little time for much discussion of the relationship between the Rolemap and the real world, there should always be some effort to focus participants in this direction. After all, why else did you design the Rolemap and why did they participate in it? Also useful for participants as a follow-up activity is a handout prepared to relate the Rolemap activity to the instructional objectives and, hence, to the real world. While this could be a lengthy bibliography or series of follow-up activities, it can also be a one-page handout of questions.

Participants in *Playing Your Way Through School* were given the following handout:

*Having participated in several simulated meetings on the topic of simulations and games—all in a setting much like your own university, can you now answer these questions?*

- *What do you think the major complaints of your faculty will be?*
- *How will you answer these complaints?*
- *Which departments do you think will be most accepting of S/G? Most opposed to S/G?*
- *Which individuals do you think might be most supportive? Most opposed?*
- *What help can you offer in the selection of S/G for different academic disciplines?*

- *What training opportunities in S/G can you offer interested faculty?*
- *What steps can you take to inform the faculty (the students, the parents) so that the kind of negative criticism and rumors stirred up by the newspaper article can be avoided?*

6. *Prepare and debug prototype on convenient audience.* The only truly effective way to find the weaknesses and errors in your Rolemap is to try it out. No matter how carefully you analyze, select, write, or edit, you almost certainly will miss something which will show up—to the loss of instructional effectiveness and to your embarrassment—in the use of the Rolemap with a group of participants. Hence, for your sake, as well as for your participants, try your Rolemap with a group of relatives, friends, or co-workers.

Have a clean script and read the narrative which will later be recorded on an audiotape. Keep time so that discussion time can be adjusted and also so that you will have an estimate of total time needed. Type role descriptions and provide each player with his or her own individual booklet or pages. The booklet may just be stapled together. It is amazingly easy to assemble the wrong roles in players' booklets, e.g., having the same player assigned the neutral role throughout, so such a trial can be invaluable.

If you cannot get a group together for the complete Rolemap, at least do an abbreviated version, i.e., give the introduction and first set-up, have people read their roles and begin the discussion of Session I, then abort Session I and move on to Session II, once again having them read their roles and begin the discussion phase. Continue through the last session in this fashion. By doing this kind of tryout, you should eliminate any major problems in role assignments, continuity, role conflicts or imbalances, and other general procedures. If possible, have a helper who records errors— typographical, grammatical, labeling, and other trivial as well as major errors. Such a written record will be useful in revising the Rolemap.

If your "convenient" audience is not really representative, the most difficult part of a Rolemap to try out will be the debriefing section, which requires not only the experience of the entire Rolemap, but also the expertise and background which bona fide participants bring to the activity.

The primary purpose of this "tryout" step is to debug the Rolemap, i.e., to eliminate mechanical errors which could interfere with the effectiveness of the Rolemap. Such a tryout can be done with very little investment of time and should be considered an absolute minimum "evaluation" effort before use.

7. *Try out on representatives of target population.* The purpose of this higher-level tryout is to evaluate the instructional effectiveness of the design so that improvements can be made. A competent trainer or instructional designer has an obligation to clients to take some steps to insure the adequacy of instruction. While not the only method, formative evaluation and revision is one of the surest means of instructional improvement. But, formative evaluation does take time. And time is money. So how much evaluation must be done? Unfortunately, there is no simple answer to that question. The number of cycles of tryout and revision that is necessary is related to factors such as (1) the designer's experience with the technique and the target population; (2) the degree of tolerable error in attaining specific instructional outcomes; (3) the probable difficulty of the subject matter for the learners; and (4) the feasibility of revision of a particular Rolemap.

The kinds of formative evaluation are several (e.g., criterion-referenced, goal-free, etc.), and the topic is too complex to enter into here. Suffice it to say that evaluation procedures and instruments commonly in use for other types of instructional strategies may be used (perhaps with some adaptations) for Rolemaps; the benefits which are commonly observed to be obtainable in other types of instructional development should be expected in Rolemap development also.

Surely, one tryout on a representative group should be attempted in any meaningful instructional project.

**Production Activities**

The tangible products of a final version of a Rolemap may or may not be "slick," i.e., professionally finished like a commercially marketed product. The degree of slickness decided upon depends on many factors—extent of expected use, marketing goals, development time, and money available. Usually, slickness has little to do with instructional effectiveness. However, if a Rolemap's intended audience will accept only slick products, then slickness may affect instructional effectiveness. (It is the author's belief that this is seldom really the case.) Also, occasionally, those who okay a budget for development cannot accept the final product unless it is a slick one. Since generally the major real cost involved is that of personnel time spent in development, for a proportionately small, additional cost—particularly if existent organizational production facilities can be used—an impressive-looking final product can be achieved. In any event, instructionally effective Rolemaps have been made with nothing more than a typewriter, a felt-tip pen, a copy machine, a stapler, and a portable audiocassette recorder.

Regardless of the level of slickness, a Rolemap should include (1) an audiotape recording, (2) role description booklets or cards and role labels, and (3) a leader's guide.

1. *Prepare final audiotape.* The audiotape can be as simply done as that recorded on a portable cassette recorder by a friend or associate with a pleasant voice. In general, the unobtrusive narrator is better than the overly dramatic reader. Background noises in the recording room should be

avoided. You may find it useful to read a section on how-to-record in some standard reference (e.g., Kemp, 1975, pp. 153-161). If a commercial quality audiotape is required, a higher quality 1/4" tape recorder can be used in a professional sound studio with professional narrators.

2. *Prepare final role description booklets or cards and role labels.* In a Rolemap with only two sessions, the simplest format is a single page (preferably of a paper of card stock weight) with the role description for Session I on one side and the role description for Session II on the other. Furthermore, this card can be folded and placed upright on the table (see Figure 11), so that while the role player can read his or her role description, other role players can read his or her name and title. Different colors can be used for Players A, B, C, D, and E. This is particularly helpful to the leader in sorting out materials for a multi-group Rolemap activity.

When a Rolemap has more than two sessions, a booklet is recommended. This booklet can be as simple as a stack of pages stapled together, with the role description for Session I first, for Session II next, and so forth. However, with only a bit more invested, a more attractive and a more durable booklet can be made by using heavier paper (card stock weight) and a spiral plastic binder (see Figure 12a). If the roles are kept to about one-third of a typewritten page as suggested earlier, a single page (8½ x 11) can be cut in half. Such a booklet lends itself to being stood up on the table—just like the single, folded card described above.

When a multi-session booklet is used for role descriptions, there are a number of ways to handle the correlated labels necessary for each session. If only one group of people is using the Rolemap, the leader can pass out the name labels for each session (and these labels can be made in numerous ways). However, this is never an overly successful procedure, since often the labels get mixed up. It is usually better to

*Figure 11*

*Role Description and Label
for a Two-Session Rolemap*

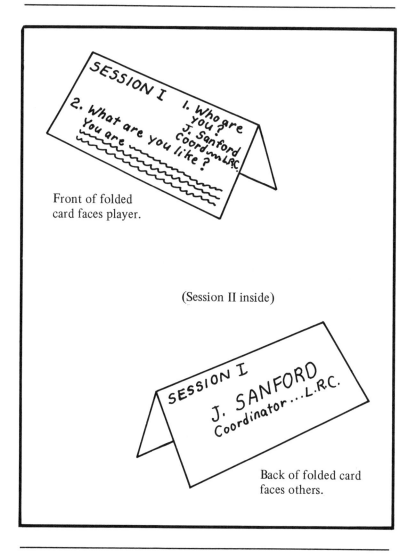

Front of folded
card faces player.

(Session II inside)

Back of folded card
faces others.

*Figure 12*

**Role Booklets and Labels
for Multi-Session Rolemaps**

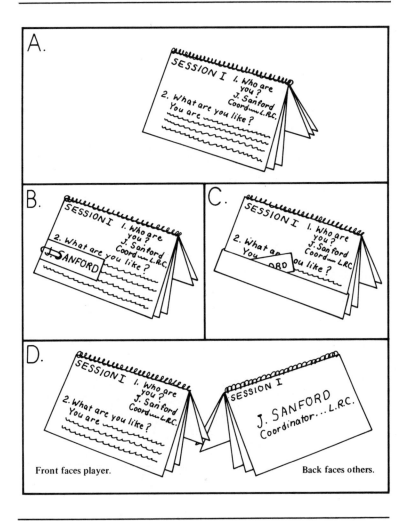

include the labels with the roles so that each player gets a complete role package. Role labels can be attached to the appropriate pages of the role booklet with paper clips (see Figure 12b) or placed in pockets (see Figure 12c), which can be made by folding the booklet page up and gluing in place. Role labels can be written on cards with a string like a necklace or on stick-on name tags from any office supplier.

The author's preferred way of dealing with role labels in a multi-session Rolemap is much like that of the two-session Rolemap. Errors may occur in production, but it is much cleaner in implementation. The role labels for each session can be placed on the backs of the pages in the role booklets so that while one player is reading his or her role description, the other players are reading the name and title of the same role (see Figure 12d).

3. *Prepare leader's guide.* For reasons of effective implementation, as well as replicability, a leader's guide should be developed. At a minimum, it should include the complete audiotape script and the debriefing questions. The script is essential in case the audio equipment fails and the leader must substitute. And, regardless of the leader's expertise, the debriefing questions are desirable as a checklist, if not direct guide, to the planned-for coverage of the instructional domain. In addition to these two elements, a leader's guide could well include the following:

- target population specifications,
- instructional goals and objectives,
- equipment and room requirements,
- step-by-step instructions for leading, and
- role descriptions for each session.

The critical parts of a leader's guide will have been developed in the course of the Rolemap development and, hence, little additional work is involved in producing this last, very useful component.

## Reference

Kemp, J.E. *Planning and Producing Audiovisual Materials* (3rd ed.). New York: Thomas Y. Crowell, 1975.

# VI.

# RESOURCES

The Rolemap is a relatively new instructional design. The "oldest" Rolemap known to the author is Guskin and Briggs' *Upset in Polymer: An Experience in Mainstreaming,* developed in 1973 at the Indiana University Center for Innovation in Teaching the Handicapped. Sivasailam Thiagarajan was the instructional developer on that project; he has since developed or co-developed a number of Rolemaps, including *Screaming Committees,* which was one of the examples used in this book. Since 1976, staff members at Indiana University's Developmental Training Center have developed numerous Rolemaps, as well as Rolemap-simulation-game hybrids. Availability of these Rolemaps is indicated below.

For information on purchase or use of the following Rolemap, contact P. Kenneth Komoski, Educational Products Information Exchange Institute, 475 Riverside Drive, New York, New York 10027.

- *Screaming Committees.* Developed by Sivasailam Thiagarajan. This Rolemap addresses the issue of the selection of textbooks in the public schools.

For information on purchase or use of the following Rolemap, contact Melvyn I. Semmel, Indiana University, Center for Innovation in Teaching the Handicapped, Bloomington, Indiana 47401.

- *Upset in Polymer: An Experience in Main-streaming.* Developed by Samuel L. Guskin, Anne Briggs, with Sivasailam Thiagarajan as instructional developer. This Rolemap addresses the issue of integrating mildly handicapped children into the regular classroom.

For information on purchase or use of the following Rolemaps, contact the developer at Indiana University, Developmental Training Center, Bloomington, Indiana 47401.

- *Are the Joneses With You?* Developed by Vicki Pappas (DTC) and Maggie Reilly (Public Information Office, Connecticut, DD Council). This Rolemap addresses philosophical issues faced by professionals, neighbors, and deinstitutionalized persons as a group home is to be established in a neighborhood.
- *Benjie: An Experience in Planning.* Developed by Vicki Pappas (DTC). This Rolemap-simulation-game is an educational adaptation of *Kenny* and simulates the process of reviewing the Individualized Educational Plan for a recently mainstreamed eight-year-old child.
- *Competence, Compatibility, and Cooperation.* Developed by Vicki Pappas and Patriciana Tracy (DTC). This Rolemap addresses the issue of building cooperative staff/parent relationships in child care centers.
- *Interdisciplinary Planning.* Developed by Vicki Pappas and Kathy Byers (DTC). This Rolemap looks at the relationship and role changes in the interdisciplinary process.
- *Interdisciplinary Planning in the Schools.* Developed by Vicki Pappas and Kathy Byers (DTC). This Rolemap looks at the relationship and role

changes as school personnel engage in interdisciplinary planning in response to P.L. 94-142 mandates.

- *Kenny: Planning for an Individual.* Developed by Michael Tracy, Diane Dormant, Tessa Durham, Vicki Pappas, and Suzanne Sturgeon (DTC). This Rolemap-simulation-game looks at the process of planning an Individualized Habilitation Plan for a young, recently deinstitutionalized adult.
- *Technical Assistance.* Developed by Suzanne Sturgeon and Michael Tracy. This Rolemap explores various models of providing technical assistance.

In addition to custom-designing Rolemaps for individual organizational applications, Diane Dormant presents an overview of Rolemaps in a two- to three-hour session and training in the production of Rolemaps in a one- to two-day workshop. She can be contacted at 4412 E. Trailridge Road, Bloomington, Indiana 47401.

# VII.

# APPENDIX A

## Kenny: Planning for an Individual*

Developers: Michael Tracy, Diane Dormant, Tessa Durham, Vicki Pappas, Suzanne Sturgeon

The introduction and set-up to the first session of *Kenny: Planning for an Individual* were designed and developed as a sound-slide set, which provided all participants with a common case study. This sound-slide set was ultimately converted into a filmstrip for national dissemination. The script and descriptions of the pictures are presented here to illustrate this kind of audio-visual introduction to a Rolemap.

*Presented here with the permission of the Development Training Center, Indiana University, 2853 East Tenth Street, Bloomington, Indiana 47401; Henry Schroeder, Executive Director.

### Kenny: Planning for an Individual

1. Start on title slide.          Start cassette #1 (000)
                                   (No narration)

2. Picture of Kenny.              • *Narrator:* First of all to-
                                    day, I'd like to tell you
                                    something about a young
                                    man named Kenny De-
                                    witt.

                                    Kenny is 19 years old
                                    and, for the past five
                                    years—up till two months
                                    ago—he was living at

3. Eastland Hospital.             • Eastland, one of the state
                                    hospitals for the re-
                                    tarded. For the last two
                                    years of this time, he was
                                    in

4. Entrance of communi-           • their community module,
   ty module.                       being trained for place-
                                    ment back in the com-
                                    munity. Then, two
                                    months ago,

5. Kenny leaving East-            • Kenny left Eastland, on
   land.                            convalescent leave, to live
                                    in the Pine County

6. Kenny at group home.

• Group Home in Wood-
bridge, New State.

*Group Home Parent:*
Well, I guess the most
irritating thing about
Kenny is that you really
can't count on him to
follow the rules. He does
things like—well, we buy
food for the week on
Saturday, and we divide
it up—you know, every-
body has a box for his or
her week's snacks. Well,
if I don't watch him,
Kenny will just eat everybody's stuff up in the
first few days. He seems
to have a little trouble
setting limits.

7. Kenny playing records.

• One of the things Kenny
likes to do is play rec-
ords. He has his own
phonograph and his own
records, but, of course,

8. Kenny looking at rec-
ord.

• sometimes he doesn't
have just the record he
wants to hear, and, if he
wants a record Bobby
has, and Bobby's not

around to ask, Kenny just helps himself!

Still, in spite of this kind of problem, I'd have to say

9. Kenny coming upstairs.

- Kenny is a pretty likeable fellow. He offers to help me with my chores.

Sometimes, I think if we could find enough things for him to do, everything else would be just fine.

*Narrator*: Kenny is also enrolled in the work evaluation program at the Pine County Sheltered Workshop.

10. Kenny at bus stop.

- Every weekday morning at 8:30, two blocks from the Group Home, Kenny waits for the city bus to ride across town to the Workshop.

11. Bus driver.

- *Bus Driver*: I'm sorry, but, after all I was hired to drive the bus. I want to help these kids all I can, but it's just not fair to everybody else who rides this bus. I mean he just stands up whenever he takes a mind to and he wanders around the bus, talking to first this person and then to that one. I just can't have it. If he's going to ride this bus, he's got to sit down and shut up.

12. Kenny carrying packages.

- *Narrator*: Kenny's actual work evaluation hasn't begun yet at the Workshop, so most of the time he's been doing odd jobs.

13. Kenny baling hay.

- *Workshop Director*: Kenny seems like a pretty capable young man. It depends a lot upon the job he's doing. When I ask him to run errands, he can do as many as three or four things without forgetting any of them. And, too, when he likes a job, he's fast at it. Of course, the more you reinforce him, the better he works.

14. Kenny sorting.

- He does get bored, though, at routine kinds of tasks.

15. Kenny sorting.

- Take sorting, for example.

16. Kenny looking out window.

- His mind starts wandering in a hurry at the sorting table. (Chuckle) I can't say I blame him much.

17. Kenny collating.

- Or collating.

18. Kenny looking at another worker.

- He's okay for awhile,

19. Kenny looking out window.

- and then, something else looks more interesting.

20. Kenny with people.

- *Narrator*: Generally, Kenny has gotten along well with most people. Back at Eastland, he was well-liked by both the staff and the residents. And, he

21. Kenny reading with a friend.

- seems to be making friends in his new situation, too.

  *Workshop Director*: Yes, Kenny gets along pretty well with other people. That's why it surprised me when he hit those two boys last week. I'd sure like to know what that was really all about. Maybe, it's just growing up. You know, it's hard enough to grow up when you're not retarded.

22. Sample tests.

- *Narrator*: Over the years at Eastland, Kenny has taken a number of diagnostic tests. When he was 14, the Vineland showed his social maturity to be that of an eight-year-old, the Wechsler yielded an IQ of 60, and speech and hearing tests showed his hearing to be normal and his language development to be that of an eight-year-old.

23. Kenny taking test.

- Several years later, when he was 17, achievement

tests on spelling, reading, and math showed him to be at about the second grade level.

24. Kenny on bike.

- Physically, Kenny has always been well-developed.

  He spent a lot of time at Eastland outdoors. In fact, he often made the deliveries between buildings.

25. Kenny playing basketball.

- And, he was also one of their most outstanding participants in the Special Olympics, going to the Nationals for two years in a row.

26. Kenny watching television.

- *Group Home Parent*: The only time Kenny sits still to watch television is when an Indiana basketball game is on.

27. Kenny dressing.

- *Narrator*: Kenny's self-help skills are generally quite good. However, he

does sometimes need re-
minders about personal
hygiene.

*Group Home Parent*: He
can be a bit haphazard
about being clean. If I
didn't tell him to, I'm
not sure he would ever
take a bath. I don't
know, maybe that's how
he was raised.

28. Kenny's home.

• I really don't know much
about his background.
I've only met his mother
twice. She has two
younger children at
home, although I've
never seen them. Kenny
doesn't seem to like them
very much—especially
George, his brother.

Sometimes I wonder if he
likes his mother, the way
he acts around her. You
can't blame him, though.
She treats him like such a
kid.

29. Hardware store.

• *Narrator*: Kenny's mother, Mae Dewitt, works

full-time in a hardware store. She and her husband were divorced when Kenny was nine, and Mr. Dewitt has had no further contact with the family.

30. School playground.

- Kenny's brother and sister both go to the same public school special education classes that Kenny used to go to when he lived at home.

Kenny was sent to Eastland because

31. Kenny watching children.

- he had frightened several younger children, and he was also said to have killed some small animals. His mother and his teachers did not feel they could control him any longer.

At Eastland, while Kenny occasionally had an outburst and broke something, he was never again known to hit or attack a person. While there, he was put on tranquilizers, and he is still taking them.

32. Kenny looking at a magazine.

- *Group Home Parent*: The only other important thing I might mention about Kenny is that he seems to be developing some pretty typical interest in girls and sex and so forth.

  There's one girl in particular that he likes. She's at the Workshop, too. I think he would like to ask her for a date, but he hasn't figured out just how to go about it yet.

33. Kenny on porch.

- *Narrator*: Kenny Dewitt has been back in the community for two months now.

34. Planning session diagram.

  (graphic showing five people around a table)

- Three days after he moved to the Group Home, Kenny's Planning Team met to develop an individual plan for him.

35. Highlight the name "Kenny."

- Kenny attended the meeting . . .

36. Highlight the name "Susan Smith."

- As did one of his Group Home parents, Susan Smith . . .

37. Highlight the name "Jack Bartlett."

- Plus the Director of the Sheltered Workshop, Jack Bartlett . . .

38. Highlight the name "Frances Jones."

- Also, the Regional Supervisor of Vocational Rehabilitation, Frances Jones . . .

39. Highlight the name "Carol Marshall."

- And, the community worker from Eastland State Hospital, Carol Marshall. It was she who chaired that initial meeting.

40. Minutes of the meeting.

- These are the minutes she wrote up and mailed to all the participants.

41. Minutes—highlight names of participants.

- Notice that, in addition to the five people who

were present at that
meeting, two others were
invited but unable to at-
tend: Mae Dewitt,
Kenny's mother, and
Frederick Craig, Program
Director of the Pine
County Association for
Retarded Citizens.

42. Minutes—highlight
agenda.

• The agenda for that initial meeting was:

*First*: To collect and
share information
about concerns re-
garding Kenny.

*Second*: To develop an
individual plan for
Kenny to address
those concerns—a
plan which speci-
fies:

• DESIRED OUT-
COMES,

• RESOURCES to
reach those out-
comes, and a

• REVIEW procedure
to evaluate the prog-
ress being made to-
ward those • out-
comes.

Note that the next meeting is set for May 17, at 3:30 p.m., in the Pine County Public Library conference room. And also, notice that Carol Marshall will contact those who attended the first meeting, as well as some others.

(Lights On)

43. Blank slide.

• The purpose of the second meeting of Kenny Dewitt's Planning Team will be to review the concerns stated in the individual plan which were developed at the first meeting and to decide whether to revise them, continue them, or to develop some new concerns.

Let's pause now and consider what your role is in this task today. Each of you has been asked to be a member of Kenny's Planning Team. Several

weeks ago, Carol Marshall
sent you a letter inform-
ing you of the second
meeting. In a pile in front
of you are some player
booklets. Take one and
open it to the first page
where you will see her
letter to you. Take a few
minutes now to find out
who you are and to read
that letter.

(*Note*: The transition is made here from the audio-visual
introduction to print materials, much as any other
Rolemap.)

# VIII.

# APPENDIX B

**Playing Your Way Through School**
*(Script, Role Descriptions, and Labels)*
By S. Thiagarajan and D. Dormant

*Instructions for Tryout*

1. *Participants*: Try to get four people other than yourself to agree to participate in this Rolemap. If this is not possible, have one person play two roles.

2. *Introduction and Set-Ups*: Record the script on an audiocassette, either timing the pauses between sessions or planning to turn the recorder on and off manually. Or, if an audiocassette recorder is not available, simply read the script. In the latter case, you will not be able to participate yourself.

3. *Role Booklets and Labels*:

   a. *Simplest Approach*: Reproduce role descriptions and sort them into those for Player A, those for Player B, and so forth, for the three sessions. This can be done by checking the design matrix in Figure 10 in the text. Staple the three role descriptions in order for each player. Using a felt-tip pen, make role labels (name and title). Sort the three role labels in the same order and staple them together (e.g., in top left-hand corner) so they can be folded over as used. Instruct the players (after the introduction and first set-up) to lay their labels on the table in front of them so other players can read them.

   b. *"Slicker" Approach*: Reproduce and make labels as

above. Sort as above. Go to a reproduction facility which will copy front and back for you. Assemble both the role descriptions and the role labels for each player so that you can be certain of which role labels go on the back of which role descriptions. This is tricky to get right. Assemble them with paper clips before having them copied. Then, get a card stock (heavy paper) for the outside covers and have the entire booklet punched to accept a plastic, spiral binder. Now, each player can set up his or her booklet and, as he or she turns to a new role description, display his or her label to others on the back of the turned page. (Note that this method necessitates a cover page which can be turned to reveal the label of the first role.)

## Script

### Introduction

Hello. Welcome to this workshop event. I'm going to be your guide through a series of discussions on the topic of simulations and games for college instruction.

In order to participate in this activity, you should be seated in groups of five. Each group will engage in a series of role-play activities.

In each activity, you will take on a different role. In a few minutes, you will receive a booklet which will tell you *who to be* and *what to do.* But, first, let me describe the situation in your first role-play activity.

### Set-Up for Session I (Continued from Introduction)

As the story opens, we are in the office of the Coordinator of the Learning Resources Center, J. Sanford. Sanford just returned from a workshop on simulations and games and is exploring the implementation of these techniques with the faculty. Sanford has invited the chairpersons of faculty departments to a meeting to discuss these techniques.

Upon his return last week, he distributed copies of the Workshop Manual to each chairperson. His goal for this meeting is to hear what they think about simulations and games as cost-effective instructional techniques for Globe University.

When you get your booklet, read the general role-play instructions on the first page. Then turn to Session I on the next page to see who you are. Read about yourself and set your booklet up so others can tell who you are. Okay, Coordinator Sanford, let's see what kind of facilitator you are in getting your faculty to loosen up and discuss their real concerns and opinions about the implementation of simulations and games. You have ten minutes. Ready? Begin.

**Set-Up for Session II**

I hope you had a lively discussion. Let's find out about the next situation. One week after the first meeting, Coordinator Sanford sent department chairpersons a memo countersigned by the Academic Vice President. The memo strongly suggested that they select and try out a simulation/game in their classes.

A month has gone by since this memo went out. By now many department heads have used a simulation/game in their own classrooms. Even the students are talking about simulations and games. In fact, some of the students have been doing quite a bit of talking! *The Globe University Gazette* sent its star reporter, McCullough, to the student lounge to interview students on the topic of simulations and games as instructional techniques.

Turn to Session II in your booklet to see who you are now. Read about your new role and set up your new name. (Pause.) Reporter McCullough, you have about ten minutes. Ready? Begin.

**Set-Up for Session III**

Welcome back. I hope you're getting into this role-playing business by now. The next activity should be an interesting one.

The campus newspaper carried a lead article on simulations and games as instructional techniques. While the article attempted to be objective, some of the quotations from students and faculty have been used out of context to generate a lot of talk. Concern has been expressed all the way up to the President of the University. Today, Academic Vice President Tracy has called a meeting to clarify the problems and to decide what, if any, actions are needed. Vice President Tracy has invited the Coordinator of the Learning Resources Center, as well as faculty and student representatives.

Open your booklet to Session III to see who you are, read about your role, and set up your name. (Pause.)

Ready Vice President Tracy? Begin.

**Concluding Comments**

Well, have you had about enough of role playing for the time being? Okay, then, the time has come to look back at your experiences and share some of your feelings, concerns, or insights. I'll be leaving you now with your workshop leader. Goodbye from Globe University.

*Role Descriptions and Labels*

-------------------------------------------------------------------

**SESSION I**                              1. Who are you?

                                           J. SANFORD
                                           Coordinator
                                           Learning Resources Center
                                           Globe University

2. What are you like?

You are the Coordinator of the Learning Resources Center at Globe University. The President has suggested that if you want promotion and tenure, the Learning Resources Center must take a major role in reducing the dropout rate, particularly during the first two years of college.

Therefore, you have been exploring new techniques which are motivationally, instructionally, and financially effective. Recently, you went to a one-week workshop on Instructional Simulations and Games. You received a lot of information and participated in a number of simulations/games.

In general, you were stimulated by the workshop, and you're interested in exploring ways to get simulations and games used appropriately in your university. In order to generate faculty interest, you distributed copies of the 400-page Workshop Manual to all department chairpersons last week. You have invited them to this meeting to discuss some of their thoughts and concerns.

3. How can you begin?

a. Since J. Rodriguez from the Language Department is new to the faculty, introduce him to the group and ask the others to introduce themselves.

b. Say why you called this meeting.

c. If the discussion doesn't get underway on its own, ask some broad questions relevant to simulations and games.

--------------------------------------------------------------------

**SESSION I**

1. Who are you?

J. RODRIGUEZ
Chairperson
Language Department
Globe University

2. What are you like?

You are new to the faculty at Globe University. You have had five years of successful teaching at a very progressive and expensive college.

You like to try new things. In fact, your application and development of new instructional techniques in your own field are the reasons you got this job. But you realize that traditional faculty members do not always like your innovativeness, and Globe has a reputation for being traditional. However, through establishing good relations with other chairpersons, you hope to have an impact on the University's teaching techniques.

You skimmed the Simulations/Games Workshop Manual, which the Coordinator of the Learning Resources Center sent to you, and you find some of the ideas quite relevant to your field. Specifically, S/G seem appropriate to accomplishing such basic goals as improving vocabulary and spelling and such high-level goals as teaching citizens the skills necessary to affect what their newspapers print. You are ready to try out S/G in your classroom.

------------------------------------------------------------------

**SESSION I**

1. Who are you?

G. NAVARRO
Chairperson
Mathematics
  Department
Globe University

2. What are you like?

You have been teaching mathematics at Globe University for 15 years. You have been Chairperson of the Mathematics Department for ten years. You like things the way they are and have little patience with outsiders and their ideas. You don't care if they want to play around in literature and political science classes.

Mathematics is a serious subject, and you know how to teach it. Give good, solid lectures. Give plenty of homework. Allow five minutes at the end of each class for questions. Be available three hours a week in your office to see students. Get tests graded and back as soon as possible. That's how to teach!

You never did care much for mollycoddling students. Sanford is a pleasant person, but that whole Learning Resources Center is just a way to spoonfeed lazy students, and if Sanford thinks you have time to read a 400-page book on silliness, Sanford is crazy.

-------------------------------------------------------------------

**SESSION I**

1. Who are you?

H. KENT
Chairperson
Political Science
    Department
Globe University

2. What are you like?

You are the Head of the Political Science Department at Globe University. You are a relatively independent person, but one who takes others' opinions and needs into account. You have a secure position in your field and in this university, and you like both the teaching and the administrative ends of your job.

You had been a bit curious about what simulations and games might have to offer the Political Science Department since you heard about them at a convention last year. However, after trying to wade through that 400-page Workshop Manual on simulations and games, you are not so sure. There seems to be a lot involved just in learning how to find and use materials which are already developed. You had been particularly interested in developing some things of your own, but unless they'll give you the semester off, that doesn't seem possible. You are overwhelmed and discouraged.

--------------------------------------------------------------------

**SESSION I**

1. Who are you?

M. BOYD
Chairperson
Business Department
Globe University

2. What are you like?

You are the Head of the Business Department at Globe University. Your primary interest is in accounting. You think playing games wastes the time you need to teach accounting. Furthermore, you believe that if your faculty wants to learn new ways to teach, it's up to them. They don't tell you how to teach and you don't tell them how. And everybody is happy.

You glanced over the 400-page Workshop Manual on simulations and games which Sanford sent you. You came to this meeting with a number of comments to make which should put a stop to this whole idea—at least in your department: (1) The curriculum is well-developed and detailed in every business course. There is no time for fancy new ways to do things which waste valuable time. (2) Accounting, in particular, is a matter of learning procedures and practicing them. Group activities cannot help. (3) You and your faculty have very precise, tested ways of evaluating students. Simulations and games are impossible to evaluate. How would you know whether a student was doing anything or goofing off?

-------------------------------------------------------------------

**SESSION II**

1. Who are you?

A. SMITH
Student from an
    Economics Class
Globe University

2. What are you like?

You are a sophomore student at Globe University. You are an average student and as yet have not decided what you want to do when you graduate. If it weren't for your father, you might drop out of college. The teachers don't seem to care what you do. They get paid no matter what happens.

Take what happened last week. That Economics teacher must have forgotten to prepare for class. All period the teacher just walked around and watched while the students fiddled around, playing some sort of game. "Economic System" he called it. And, after a whole period of trying to get the rules straight, nothing much had happened, and the teacher said, "Oh, well, I guess you can't play this game in one hour." You never did know what was going on, but then no one else did either.

If you had your way, you'd look at films more. When you have films, you feel like you learn a lot. If they're going to do something different, you wish they'd show films.

-------------------------------------------------------------------

**SESSION II**

**2. What are you like?**

You are a senior at Globe University, and your major subject and interest in school is journalism. You are the best reporter on the University newspaper, *The Globe University Gazette*. The Editor called you in yesterday and suggested that you follow up some leads on a new kind of instruction which had reached the campus.

According to the Editor, several people have called the newspaper about something called "Simulations and Games." One call came from a parent who said her son called home to say they were playing a game all week in one class. Another call came from a faculty member who asked to remain anonymous but who said that the administration was trying to tell him how to teach.

1. Who are you?

M. McCULLOUGH
Newspaper Reporter
*The Globe University
Gazette*

3. How can you begin?

a. Since the group may not know each other, ask the members to give their names and the class in which they have experienced a simulation and game.

b. Say why you invited them to this meeting.

c. If the discussion doesn't get underway on its own, ask some broad questions relevant to simulations and games.

The Editor has assigned you to do a lead story but first to interview some students. You began by reading a little about instructional simulations and games in the library, and now you have invited several students who have experienced classroom simulations or games to join you in a group interview in the Student Union. You hope to find out today just how the students feel about simulations and games, and why.

------------------------------------------------------------------

**SESSION II**

2. What are you like?

You are a sophomore student at Globe University. Your major is accounting, and you had hoped to go into banking upon graduation. However, lately you have been seriously considering dropping out of college. It all seems so irrelevant to the real world. Sometimes you wonder if you are learning anything. It's just like more high school.

In fact, the most interesting thing that has happened in the past two years of college is what happened last week. In one of your business courses, you played a computerized game on how to operate a company efficiently and ethically and still make a profit. You learned something about how a firm operates. You also learned how to improve group inter-

1. Who are you?

C. MASON
Student from a Business Class
Globe University

actions and to make decisions which were good for the company and for the workers.

And, for the first time, you got to talk to some of the other people in the class. Two of the people on your team are interested in a lot of the same things you are, and you've already had one study session together. You're in favor of more activities like this one.

-----------------------------------------------------------------------

**SESSION II**

2. What are you like?

You are a freshman in Globe University, and you don't know in what discipline you want to major. However, you are determined to take all the basic courses required for just about any major so you will be safe. You have always received good grades at school. You attended a fairly demanding and very traditional high school. You really never question anything. You do what is expected.

You do not like what happened last week in your mathematics class. The teacher suddenly announced that you would form small groups and play a mathematics game. Of all the silly, childish, embarrassing things to do. You really hated it. Having to talk to all those people you didn't know. And, worse yet, having to waste your time with their ignorance. Really!

1. Who are you?

D. RUSSELL
Student from a Mathematics Class
Globe University

You certainly hope there will be no more of that kind of thing. You didn't come to college to play games. Leave that for the football team.

---

**SESSION II**

1. Who are you?

F. POWERS
Student from a Political Science Class
Globe University

2. What are you like?

You are a liberal arts junior. You want to go on to some kind of graduate school; but you haven't yet decided what kind. Probably psychology or law, although you are taking all the science courses required for medical school.

You enjoy reading and the people you have met in the university, including some faculty with whom you've become friends. You are curious about new things and enjoyed the simulation last week. All the students got really involved. The three-hour class period went by very rapidly. And, for the first time, the discussion period near the end was exciting, and a lot of people talked about their feelings and frustrations. Also, you suspect that some people, who had never thought about it, began to see how it feels to be the underdog.

For understanding social problems and people's feelings, you're convinced that simulations can be very valuable and interesting teaching techniques.

You're planning on using this one yourself in the summer camp in which you
teach.

----------------------------------------------------------------

**SESSION III**                        1. Who are you?

                                       R. RESTON
                                       Representative from
                                           the Student Union
                                       Globe University

2. What are you like?

You are a senior at Globe University, and
you have held many student offices.
Today you are the person chosen from
the Board of the Student Union to
represent the positive point of view with
regard to the use of simulations and
games as instructional techniques at
Globe University.

You are a conscientious person, and you
have collected a number of positive opinions from students. It is these positive-
position students whom you represent
today.

Spend a few seconds thinking of every
reason you can why simulations and
games are *appropriate and useful* in college courses.

----------------------------------------------------------------

**SESSION III**                        1. Who are you?

                                       V. PAPPAS
                                       Representative from
                                           the Student Union
                                       Globe University

2. What are you like?

You are a senior at Globe University, and you have held many student offices. Today you are the person chosen from the Board of the Student Union to represent the negative point of view with regard to the use of simulations and games as instructional techniques at Globe University.

You are a conscientious person, and you have collected a number of negative opinions from students. It is these nega-tive-position students whom you repre-sent today.

Spend a few seconds thinking of every reason you can why simulations and games are *inappropriate* for college use.

---

**SESSION III**

2. What are you like?

You are the Vice President for Academic Affairs, and you answer to the Board regarding instruction at Globe University. Recently, you supported the efforts of Sanford in trying to introduce the faculty to a new technique—simulations and games. But things seem to have taken a bad turn.

The university newspaper carried an arti-cle under the headline "Playing Your Way

1. Who are you?

M. TRACY
Vice President,
    Academic Affairs
Globe University

3. How can you begin?

a. Since the students and the faculty may not know each other, introduce each person and the group he or she represents.

b. Say why you called this meeting.

Through School." Your office has had five phone calls from out-of-town parents, and the President's Office has had three.

Still, you're used to staying calm in the face of trouble. Furthermore, Globe University needs all the good instructional techniques it can get, and you want to give instructional simulations and games a fair test. Therefore, you have called Sanford as well as student and faculty representatives to a meeting to discuss the use of instructional simulations and games in Globe's classrooms.

c. If the discussion doesn't get underway on its own, ask some broad questions relevant to simulations and games.

-------------------------------------------------------------------

**SESSION III**

2. What are you like?

You are the person most responsible for bringing instructional simulations and games to Globe University, and you are convinced that they are useful. You are also aware that some faculty and students are threatened by even the words "simulations" and "games," let alone by techniques which get teachers out from behind their podiums and students interacting with each other.

You hope to provide the Vice President with realistic and accurate answers to any questions and to overcome any objections which the extremists have. Spend a few

1. Who are you?

J. SANFORD
Coordinator
Learning Resources
   Center
Globe University

seconds thinking of every reason you can why simulations and games are *appropriate and useful* in college courses.

-----------------------------------------------------------------

**SESSION III**

1. Who are you?

G. NAVARRO
Chairperson
Mathematics
    Department
Globe University

2. What are you like?

Well, you were negative about trying out such foolishness as simulations and games in your math classes, and you are still negative.

In fact, now you have proof that they won't work in classes like mathematics and science, where there are real facts to teach. After all, you tried one out, didn't you? And, just as you thought, it didn't work. The class even agreed with you. It was a waste of time.

Spend a few seconds to think of every reason you can why simulations and games are *inappropriate*, not only for mathematics courses but for all college courses.

-----------------------------------------------------------------

DIANE DORMANT has a Ph.D in instructional systems technology from Indiana University and an M.A. in psychology from the University of Houston. She taught in college and public schools for 15 years and currently is an independent consultant in training and instructional development, working for a variety of organizations—in industry, education, and government. She has designed or conducted over one hundred training workshops on small-group techniques (e.g., Rolemaps, Frame Games, simulations), collaborative planning, instructional design, and change agentry. She has developed a wide variety of instructional materials, including Rolemaps, simulations, Frame Games, audio-visual packages, and print materials.